Geodetic Astrology for Relocating and World Affairs

Chris McRae

The Wessex Astrologer

Published in 2016 by
The Wessex Astrologer Ltd,
4A Woodside Road
Bournemouth
BH5 2AZ
www.wessexastrologer.com

© Chris McRae 2016

Chris McRae asserts the moral right to be recognised as
the author of this work.

Cover Design by Jonathan Taylor
Nelson Mandela voting in 1994, credit to Paul Weinburg
Man on Moon, credit to NASA/James B. Irwin
Steve Jobs, credit to Matthew Yohe

A catalogue record for this book is available at The British Library

ISBN 9781910531181

All charts and maps produced using Solar Fire Gold v.8

No part of this book may be reproduced or used in any form or by any means without the written permission of the publisher. A reviewer may quote brief passages.

CONTENTS

List of Illustrations   v

Introduction   vii

Chapter 1 Definition of Geodetic Equivalents   1
    How to Compute Charts   1
    Geodetic Reference Map   4
    Ancient Ptolemaic Country Rulerships   5

Chapter 2 Geodetic Country and City Rulerships   8
    National and Locality Geodetic Identities   8
    Similarities of Geodetic Coordinates with Ptolemaic Rulerships   13
    Geodetic Cusps: Major Cities in the United States   14
    Geodetic Cusps: Major Cities of the World Excluding the US   17

Chapter 3 Relocational Geodetic Charts and Maps   24
    Planetary Influences   26
    John F. Kennedy: Relocated with Eclipse Charts   28
    Lee Harvey Oswald: Relocated with Eclipse Charts   29
    Application of the Geodetic Map: Sir Edmund Hillary   30
    General George Patton Geodetic Chart and Map   32
    Steve Jobs Geodetic Chart and Map   34

Chapter 4 Geophysical Disruptions   37
    Earthquakes   40
    Eclipses in Forecasting Earthquakes   43
    The Great San Francisco Earthquake   47
    The Great Chilean Earthquake   49
    Good Friday Alaskan Earthquake   51
    Earthquakes in Japan   53
    Niigata Japan Earthquake   55
    Anatolian Fault in Turkey   56
    Mexico City Earthquake   56
    Sumatra Indian Ocean Mega Earthquake and Tsunami   58
    The Great Tohoku Earthquake of 2011   60
    Volcanic Activity   62
    Eruption of Eyjafjallajökull Volcano   63
    Mount Saint Helens Eruption   65
    Mount Pelee Eruption   67

Chapter 5 Major Storms — 71
    Hurricane Gilbert — 74
    Hurricane Katrina — 77
    Hurricane Wilma — 79
    Weather in Australia — 81
    Perth Storm — 81
    Cyclone Yasi — 82

Chapter 6 Following the Daily News — 85
    RMS Titanic Set Sail — 87
    Operation Desert Storm — 88
    Terrorist Attack of 9/11 — 89
    The Great Mutation of 1702 — 90
    Invasion of Iraq — 92
    Rwanda Genocide — 93
    The Columbine School Massacre — 94
    New York Explosion — 95
    Germanwings Airbus Crash — 96
    1929 Stock Market Crash — 97

Chapter 7 Summary of Making Geodetic Predictions — 100

Chapter 8 Guide for Construction of a Geodetic World Map — 103

Bibliography — 107

LIST OF ILLUSTRATIONS

Figure #1	Geodetic Midheavens on a Map	2
Figure #2	Geodetic Cusps	2
Figure #3	Geodetic Reference Map	4
Figure #4	Map of Ptolemy Rulerships	5
Figure #5	John F. Kennedy Natal & Geodetic charts, Dallas, Texas	28
Figure #6	Lee Harvey Oswald Natal & Geodetic charts, Dallas, Texas	29
Figure #7	Sir Edmund Hillary Natal Chart	30
Figure #8	Sir Edmund Hillary Geodetic Planet Map	31
Figure #9	General George Patton Natal Chart	32
Figure #10	General George Patton Geodetic Planet Map	33
Figure #11	Steve Jobs Natal Chart	34
Figure #12	Steve Jobs Geodetic Planet Map	35
Figure #13	Map of Tectonic Plates of the World	41
Figure #14	Eclipse Paths	46
Figure #15	The Great San Francisco Earthquake	48
Figure #16	The Great Chilean Earthquake	50
Figure #17	The Great Alaskan Earthquake	52
Figure #18	Niigata, Japan Earthquake	54
Figure #19	Anatolian Fault Line, Turkey	56
Figure #20	Mexican City Quake of 1985	57
Figure #21	Sumatra Mega Thrust Earthquake	59
Figure #22	The Great Tohoku Earthquake	61
Figure #23	Eyjafjallajökull Eruption in Iceland	63
Figure #24	Geodetic Chart for Eyjafjallajökull Eruption	64
Figure #25	Mount Saint Helens Volcanic Eruption	66
Figure #26	Krakatoa Volcanic Eruption	68
Figure #27	Mount Pelee Volcanic Eruption	70
Figure #28	Basic Declination Graph	73
Figure #29	Hurricane Gilbert	74
Figure #30	Geodetic Wheel for Dhaka, Bangladesh	75
Figure #31	Hurricane Katrina	78
Figure #32	Hurricane Wilma	80
Figure #33	Storm in Perth, Australia	82
Figure #34	Cyclone Yasi	83
Figure #35	RMS Titanic Set Sail	87
Figure #36	Operation Desert Storm	88
Figure #37	9/11 Terrorist Attack	90
Figure #38	The Great Mutation of 1702	91
Figure #39	Invasion of Iraq	92

Figure #40	Rwanda Genocide	93
Figure #41	Columbine School Shooting	94
Figure #42	New York Gas Explosion	95
Figure #43	Germanwings Airbus Crash	96
Figure #44	Stock Market Crash of 1929	98
Figure #45	Geodetic Map Construction	106

INTRODUCTION

The Geodetic Equivalent concept of applying the signs of the zodiac across the surface of the Earth first came to my attention as a result of an innate sense of curiosity. As I studied astrology alone, isolated from other astrologers, I had only books to refer to and so I read, digested and experimented, having no-one to share ideas with, get feedback from, or to determine if I was on the right track. My membership of the American Federation of Astrologers and their catalogue of books became my lifeline to the outside world of astrology. I pored over the book list like a madman plotting some great scheme, which indeed I was. I ordered, I read voraciously, I experimented, and the result was that I developed an in-depth cross-section of astrological information and opinion.

This hunt and peck system of searching for viable astrological information sometimes led down blind alleys but at other times it unearthed little gems such as a wee publication entitled *The Geodetic Equivalent*, written under the pen name of Sepharial whose real name was Dr. Walter Gorn Old. It measured only four-and-a-half by six-and-an-eighth inches thick, was written presumably in the 1920s and reprinted by the American Federation of Astrologers in 1972. I didn't know what it was about, but the price was so minimal that I ordered it. It took no longer to read than the time it took to drink a cup of coffee, but it opened up a whole new world of exciting research. Its initial appeal was its simplicity, but as time went on I could see it had much more depth than I at first realized. I was captivated by the range of possibility.

I first learned that the Geodetic chart is simply a house cusps structure drawn up for any geographic location into which one can insert transits for the time of an event or even insert an eclipse chart to see if an area was earmarked for a special event. A natal chart can also be inserted into the Geodetic cusps for any geographic location to see where planets are angular for a relocation assessment.

It was so easy and fast to do that I found myself casting Geodetic cusps and applying transits for incidents announced during the evening newscast, and soon I had a pile on my desk waiting for me to cast the charts. I wondered if the permanent Geodetic angles could be drawn on a map of the world in order to allocate angular planetary positions. I marked the Midheavens on a map, placing the zodiac eastward from Greenwich in thirty-degree increments matching thirty degrees of longitude starting with Aries. The first thirty degrees of eastern longitude has an Aries Midheaven, the second thirty degrees has a Taurus Midheaven and so on with 29° Pisces butting up against 0° Aries after circling the globe. Drawing the Ascendant lines on a flat map surface was more time consuming. The process is outlined in the last chapter of this book.

By now I had learned enough to start presenting it to others at conferences. The first presentation was in about 1980 at The Seven Hills Conference in Lynchburg, Virginia, and then in 1982 at the American Federation of Astrologers Conference in Chicago, Illinois. In the early 1990s I recall making a presentation at the Arizona Astrological Society in Scottsdale, Arizona, which was attended by prominent astrologer and author Noel Tyl. He told me that one of the reasons he had moved to Fountain

Hills in the Phoenix area was because of the way his natal chart fitted into the Geodetic energy of the area. He has been in Phoenix ever since, which would be about twenty-five years.

As the concept was gaining popularity, we had to convince astrological programmers to include it into their computer programs. They all now include both the Geodetic charts as well as Geodetic maps showing where natal planets are angular.

And so I have come to write this book, based on all those years of intrepid research. The first manuscript was called *The Geodetic World Map* in 1988 and has long been out of print. It was also somewhat minimal in its content compared to this book.

In the following chapters you will learn that the Geodetic Equivalent has several areas of application as follows:

Personal relocation, with planets plotted on a chart or world map

Rulership of nations according to their Midheaven and Ascendant zodiacal positions

Global news such as political upheavals, geophysical activities such as earthquakes and volcanic eruptions, great storms such as tornadoes and hurricanes/cyclones, and other cataclysmic activities such as fires and floods etc.

Extreme weather activities

Along with Astro*Carto*Graphy® devised by Jim Lewis in the mid-1970s, this is another way to determine which planets are angular as we travel across the world. The main difference between the two systems is that Astro*Carto*Graphy® requires a separate map for each chart whereas the Geodetic concept has permanent angles on a map onto which planets can be applied.

Geodetic astrology may not solve all of our predictive dilemmas as we search for the perfect framework especially in the context of mundane astrology, but I hope the many examples in this book will encourage further study in this fascinating area.

CHAPTER 1

Definition of the Geodetic Equivalent (GE)

The Geodetic Equivalent concept was originally a house cusp structure calculated for any geographic location on planet Earth. A natal chart inserted within it would be used for personal relocation observing where planets would be angular for emphasis. The chart of an eclipse, lunation, or Great Conjunction could also be inserted within its cusp structure for mundane astrology, observing angular emphasis.

How to Compute Charts

The Midheaven is calculated first by laying the 360 degrees of the zodiac eastward from Greenwich beginning with 0 degrees Aries, with each zodiacal degree matching a degree of earthly longitude. This becomes the Midheaven of a chart for any particular location. Examples of a Geodetic Midheaven (MC):

    Paris Geographic Longitude 2E20
    Geodetic MC 2:20 Aries

    Moscow Geographic Longitude 37E34
    Geodetic MC 7:34 Taurus
    The first 30 degrees would be under the Aries MC

    Seoul, Korea Geographic Longitude 126E57
    126 divided by 30 = 4 complete signs (120) + 6:57
    Geodetic MC for Seoul is therefore 6:57 Leo

    San Francisco, California, Geographic Longitude 122W25
    We calculate this by going backwards in the zodiac from 0 Aries
    359:60 – 122:25 Longitude for San Francisco = 7 complete signs (210) + 27.35
    Geodetic MC for San Francisco is 27:35 Scorpio

  Refer to Figure #1 to visually see the zodiac laid out eastward from its beginning point of Greenwich. The signs from 0 to 30 degrees are marked across the top of the map and cover the complete vertical area from north to south.
  Geodetic Equivalents have also been taken from the Great Pyramid of Giza as the beginning point but popularity remains with the starting point at Greenwich from which world time zones are calculated.
  Once a Midheaven is ascertained, the other cusps can be taken manually from a Table of Houses at the latitude of the geographic location in question. Before computers this was done manually, however most computer programs can now produce a Geodetic cusp wheel for any location. Two Geodetic cusp wheels are shown on the following page. Any chosen chart can be inserted within them.

Geodetic Astrology for Relocating and World Affairs

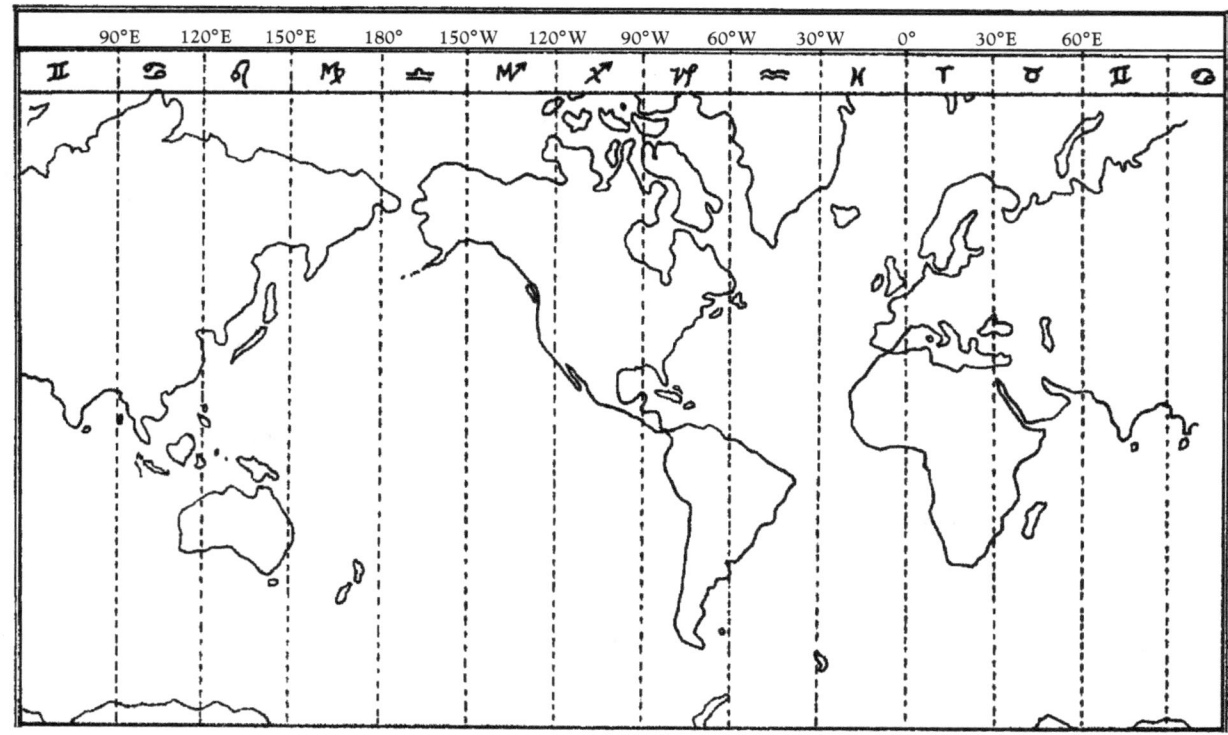

Figure #1 Geodetic Equivalent shown on a Map

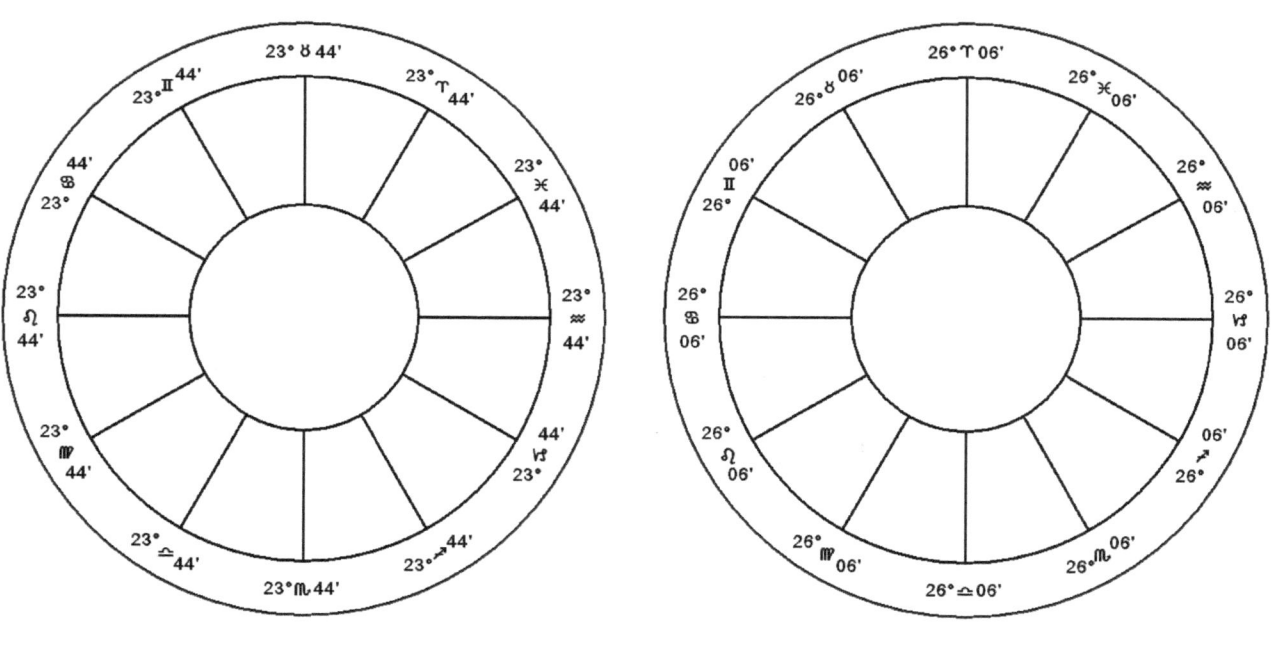

Geodetic Cusps for Moscow
37E25 55N45

Geodetic Cusps for Paris
02E20 48N52

Figure #2

Definition of the Geodetic Equivalent

After manually creating Geodetic charts for items in the news over a period of a couple of years, it seemed logical that the angles could be put on a map for quick and easy visualization of planetary influence crossing angles. Angular planets operate more overtly and visually than other positions. Drawing the intermediary cusps on a map would be much too congested. Eclipse degrees can also be followed on a Geodetic map easier than drawing up a whole chart; a Geodetic map can also be used visually for Relocation astrology. All of these will be dealt with in the following chapters.

As already indicated, the Midheavens were easily allocated on a map and the Ascendants were taken from a Table of Houses. I have used Placidus houses in this book but any chosen geometric system of preference could be used. Zero degrees of each Ascendant are noted for the corresponding Midheaven, at increasing increments of 15 degrees geographic latitude, going north and south of the equator. These Ascendant positions were plotted on a map and lines drawn to complete each Ascendant line. The Ascendants cover a specific area from east to west. A large wall map can be drawn using these coordinates as listed in Chapter 8, Guide for Instruction of a Geodetic Wall Map.

Figure #3, Geodetic Reference Map, below, shows the Ascendant positions in accordance with their Midheaven. This was printed from Sirius Software Program.

On a large wall map, the Midheaven and Ascendants can be read to about a one degree accuracy but not of course on this small scale. Make sure the wall map you use has geographic longitude and latitude marked across the top and down the side respectively. This is necessary in plotting the positions.

As already surmised, a Geodetic chart can also be turned into a Geodetic map version that most computer programs can produce, but those maps plot only Midheaven and Ascendant positions for any planet in a natal or progressed chart. Kepler Software and Solar Fire programs produce Geodetic charts and Geodetic maps for any chart. Geodetic mapping is similar to Astro*Carto*Graphy® except for one main principle. The Geodetic angles are permanent on a map and it only requires determining where any planet is angular in terms of geographic orientation. A separate Astro*Carto*Graphy® map must be drawn for each chart because it is pertinent to only one chart. It also plots angular planetary positions.

Geodetic Astrology for Relocating and World Affairs

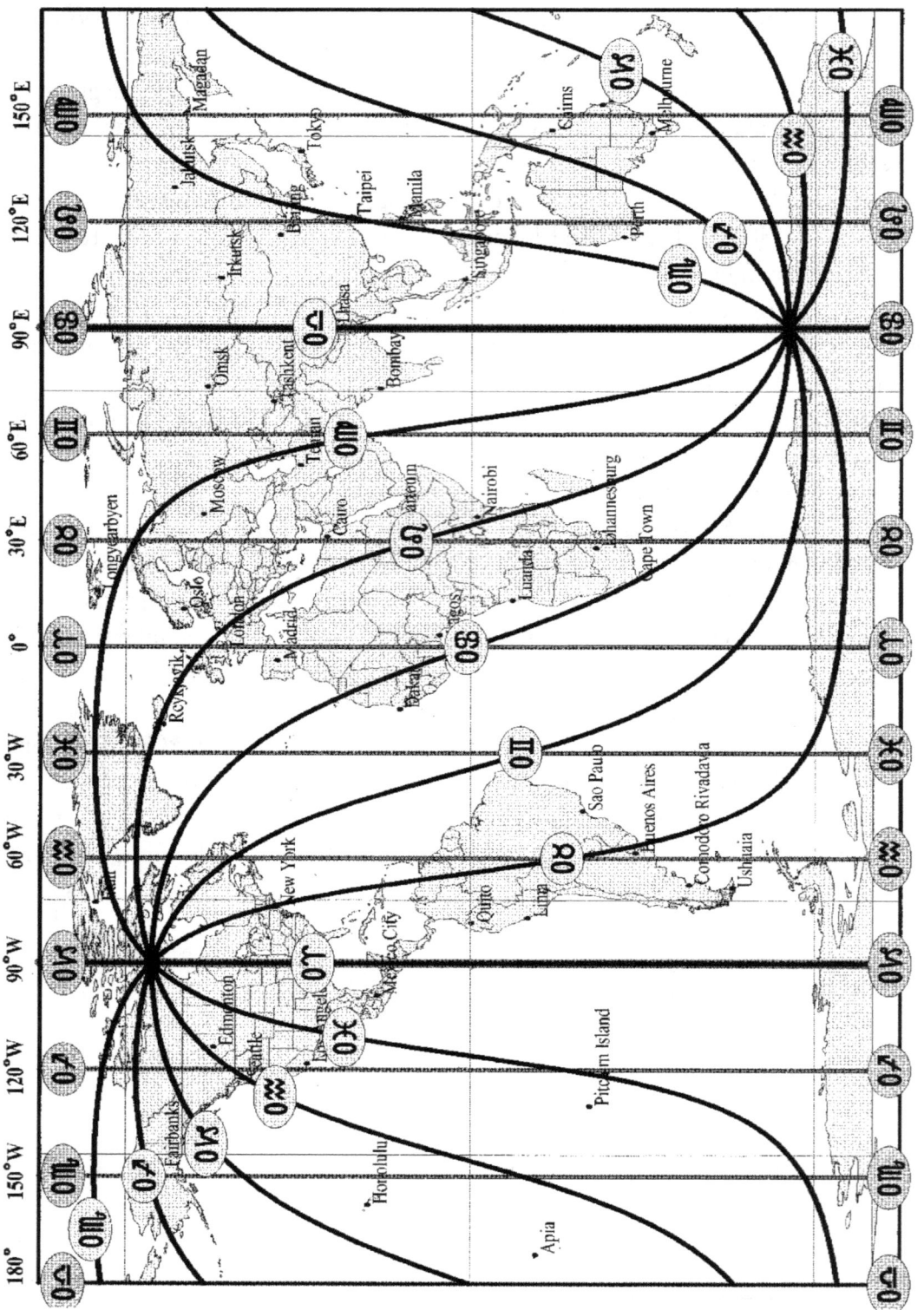

Figure #3 Geodetic Reference Map

Ancient Country Rulerships

A system of country rulerships had been devised by Ptolemy, an ancient philosopher, astrologer, geographer, and mathematician from Alexandria, 90AD to 168 AD. He is credited with devising a quadrant division to ascertain country rulerships, which is clearly laid out in the *Tetrabiblos*, his textbook of astrology. This book is still popular today and has been translated into many languages around the world.

The quadrant rulerships were based on centres of civilization and culture, however vast regions of the world were totally unknown at that time and in many cases sparsely populated. With little in the way of travel and communications, knowledge of more distant nations was limited according to the known world.

Figure #4 shows Ptolemy's old country divisions. It seems he drew a line east and west parallel to the Equator, through Gibraltar, the Mediterranean Sea, Aleppo, Iran, Afghanistan, and eastward through China. To this he added a line at right angles running north and south. The J.M. Ashmand translation of the *Tetrabiblos* creates a discrepancy as to where this north and south line was actually

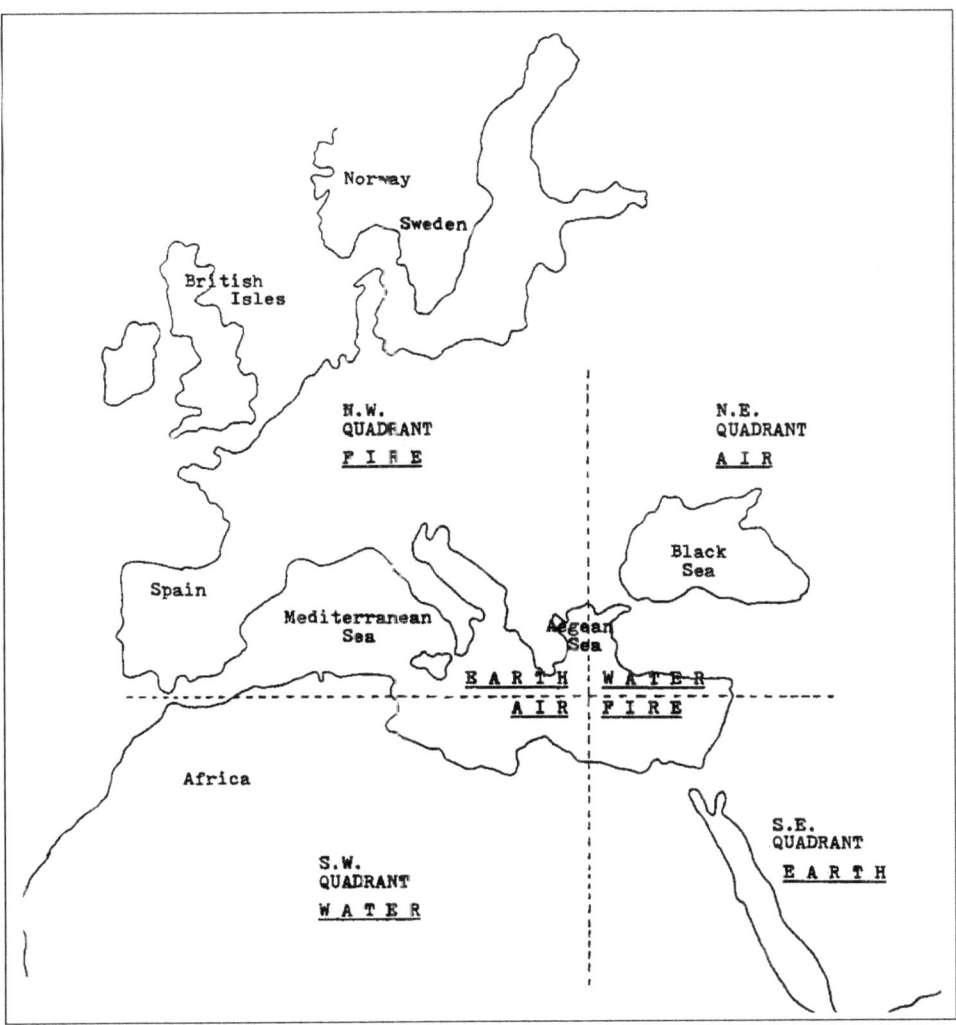

Figure #4 Map of Ptolemy Rulerships

drawn. In one line of the manuscript it says it went through "the Aegean Sea, Pontus and Lake Maeotis". Geographically on today's map this could not be a straight line and should therefore be considered to be approximate. In another line of the *Tetrabiblos* it indicates that the quadrant line went south along Eastern Africa and down between Africa and Madagascar. This would be a line north to Moscow going through Aleppo which is in today's northern Syria.

These two bisecting lines form four quadrants to which Ptolemy ascribed the four elements, Fire, Earth, Air and Water. The outer and middle extremities exemplified their appointed element but the inner parts of each quadrant were of the opposite quadrant, as follows:

North West Quadrant	Fire	Aries, Leo, Sagittarius
Inner NW Quadrant	Earth	Like Mercury, Venus, Saturn
South East Quadrant	Earth	Taurus, Virgo, Capricorn
Inner SE Quadrant	Fire	Like Mars and Jupiter
North East Quadrant	Air	Gemini, Libra, Aquarius
Inner NE	Water	Like Mars, Moon, Mercury
South West Quadrant	Water	Cancer, Scorpio, Pisces
Inner SW	Air	Like Mercury, Jupiter, Saturn

Selections were then made for groups in close proximity to the centre of the quadrant, as well as the more remote outer regions, and the middle group inbetween. The remote regions were considered less civilized and hence their signs were interpreted accordingly. For instance, the remote northwest regions such as Britain and Germany were considered to be the most fiery and warlike and hence were assigned to Aries. France and Italy being considered a bit more refined in nature were given the sign of Leo. The inner areas of this quadrant closer to the center of the earth were considered more earthly: the hedonistic Taurus group, the more "scientific" Virgo group and the "greedy" Capricorn group, to use the words translated from Ptolemy.

The outer extremities of the southeast quadrant were also attributed to the Earth element, namely Taurus, Virgo and Capricorn which are ruled by Venus, Mercury and Saturn respectively making them "lustful", "gaudy", and "of simple conduct". The inner area of this quadrant towards the middle of the earth were of the Fire element but seemingly to be somewhat "treacherous" for the Aries countries, kinder for the Leo nations, and "productive" for the Sagittarius areas.

The northeast grouping follows the same pattern, the outer extremities being of the Air element comprising countries assigned to Gemini, Libra and Aquarius, principally ruled by Saturn, Jupiter and more logically Mercury and Venus. Certain designated countries fell into the category of "rich" and "learned". The Gemini group are more apprehensive, and the Aquarian group were considered "austere" and "uncouth". The inner core of this area were of the Water element.

The outer extremities of the southwest quadrant were also composed of countries of the Water element, while the inner core were of the Air element.

This is a condensed version of the concept but I believe the point is made that these old rulerships are outdated based upon a limited geographic knowledge. Our world view both geographically and in social conduct is, of course, much broader in the 21st century.

Over the years, Ptolemy's original country rulership list has had limited revision, notably by William Lilly in the 17th century and by C.E.O. Carter in the 20th century, but a cursory study of those revisions reveals many inadequacies. Using the Geodetic Equivalent seems to make more sense and it does seem to be a better alternative. This manuscript will show how geographic locations respond to their angles, as well as how they respond to transits in the ever revolving sky above.

Another point for using the Geodetic concept for zodiacal influence of countries is that we can work visually with the permanent angles marked globally, through which most notable events occur, or we can set up whole charts for various locations as we move within a country, which allows for more fine-tuning. Take Russia for instance. The traditional rulership of Russia has changed by various authors from Ptolemy's Aquarius designation to Taurus and Sagittarius by others through time. That is understandable when we view the number of regionally different Geodetic Ascendants and Midheavens for such a large and diverse country. We can also generate charts for various cities within the country as a whole. More discussions of this will follow in the next chapter.

It would be incorrect to suggest that Ptolemy's country rulerships were all wrong. Planetary relationships have been correlated with some noteworthy events, and further observation also shows that the Geodetic Midheavens and/or Ascendants do overlap with some of the Ptolemaic versions.

CHAPTER 2

Geodetic Country and City Rulerships

If we are to accept the Geodetic Equivalent as viable country and city rulerships, we must be able to exhibit evidence to show how these localities respond to their Geodetic cusps, not only by natural and political activities occurring within their borders and boundaries, but also by national characteristics.

A large wall map with accurate Geodetic Midheavens and Ascendants plotted onto it, as described in Chapter 8, has several purposes:

Following items in the news according to angularity of planets, eclipses, lunations and even Great Conjunctions.

Visually roaming the map to observe national characteristics according to Ascendants and Midheavens of various locations and cities.

Observation of personal planets on the angles of any location in the world for quick relocation assessment.

Any size of Geodetic map can be created from the coordinates at the back of this book. Accurate plotting of Ascendants and Midheavens can only be created if longitude positions in increments of 30 degrees are indicated across the top and increments of 15 degrees of latitude are indicated along the side. A smaller version of 11"x20" or 21" can be duplicated from the *London Times Gazeteer*, from an atlas, or any map of convenient size with degrees of longitude and latitude marked accordingly. By using the coordinates given, the positions can be plotted and lines drawn showing the 30 degree range of the various Midheavens and Ascendants.

A small graphic of a Geodetic map is reproduced in Chapter 8 with instructions and a list of the coordinates for anyone to create their own. It may be useful to refer to the less cluttered map in Chapter 1 while reading the rest of this chapter. You can observe more completely the kaleidoscopic changes of nationalities as you sweep across the map, even within the borders of the same country.

The map does not eliminate setting up the whole wheel containing all the cusps for detailed work, but the scope of Geodetic work is enhanced by the map.

National and Locality Geodetic Identities

Countries and localities respond vividly to both their Geodetic Ascendant and Midheaven. The Midheaven represents how they want others to see them, their reputation and what they consider most important collectively. The Ascendant in turn represents the attitude of the people in general and how they express themselves collectively.

Our contemplative journey across the map will begin with some general observations, then focus on specific locations. These locations will be chosen at random to correlate with points of discussion.

Observe first that the larger countries have more than one Midheaven and more than one Ascendant. For example, the Russian Federation founded December 25, 1991, still occupies the largest global land mass of 17,098,242 square kilometers, stretching across a vast expanse of the earth's circumference from east to west. It is 1/8th of the world's land mass with an approximate population of 143,800,000 in 2014. How then can we justify Ptolemy's ancient designation that the sign Aquarius has rulership over such an immense territory?

Geodetically the Midheavens of Russia range over seven different signs, touching on the west by a sliver at the end of Aries, and proceeding over fertile Taurean planes, the diversified tundra regions of the Gemini and Cancer Midheaven, then across Leo and Virgo, ending with the first ten degrees of Libra at the Bering Strait, where the people live peacefully with their neighbors across a few short miles of water to the American soil of Alaska. Over the years many proposals have been made to connect the two countries by either a series of bridges or an undersea tunnel. In fact, in October 1987 the Soviet Leader, Mikhail Gorbachev, speaking in Murmansk, urged Canada to consider a treaty of Arctic cooperation with its US ally to negotiate demilitarization.

Russia also has five different Geodetic Ascendants encompassing Leo to Scorpio, exemplifying the great scope and temperament of its people.

Canada occupies the second largest land mass of the world with 9,889,000 square kilometers and a population in 2014 of only 35,675,834. As with Russia, it reflects a great diversity of what it considers important with its Midheavens of Scorpio, Sagittarius, Capricorn and Aquarius. Its Ascendants range all the way from Sagittarius to Gemini; seven in all. No wonder it has often been referred to as an extremely provincial nation with so many separate identities. It is not an easy task for a central government to orchestrate policy for so diversified a national attitude. The provinces adamantly defend their right to individual jurisdiction on many issues. It is easier to understand from the Geodetic perspective, without even being aware of the specific issues, why there are strong regional differences and even occasional talk of separatism both by the French-speaking Quebecois and the English-speaking people of Western Canada.

Note that the Federal Government of Canada in Ottawa falls under the appropriate Midheaven of Capricorn, as do Canada's Stock Exchange in Toronto, and the country's largest number of corporate headquarters and concentration of industrialization. The next most important financial and corporate headquarters in the country fall under a Midheaven of Scorpio and an Ascendant of Capricorn on the west coast.

The United States of America covers an area of 9,826,675 square kilometers with a population of 319,328,000 in 2014. It also falls under several Midheavens and Ascendants but not quite as many as either the Russian Federation or the Dominion of Canada. With fewer Ascendants there is a stronger national unity, but still an indication of several distinct national images and attitudes; these range from the distinct eastern conservatism and traditionalism to the mid-western friendliness, then on to the west coast casuality and informality.

Note that in the United States, as in Canada, the national capital falls under the appropriate Capricorn Midheaven as does the largest industrialized area and the financial institution of Wall Street.

The west coast of the United States has some interesting influences that separate the cities of Los Angeles and San Francisco by their Midheaven of Sagittarius and Scorpio respectively, while sharing an Aquarian Ascendant. I think most observers would agree that the two cities differ greatly in temperament, Los Angeles being more free-spirited where "anything goes" and San Francisco being more seriously business orientated. This is not to suggest that Los Angeles does not take its business seriously but there is a different general attitude, a different code of dress, and different acceptable codes of conduct. San Francisco is considered the financial centre of the west coast and Los Angeles is the entertainment capital.

The old adage "go west young man and make your fortune" becomes even more amusing when we observe that it falls under the influence of a Sagittarius Midheaven.

China is the fourth largest country in the world showing great diversity from east to west with three different Geodetic Midheavens and three different Ascendants. The greatest poverty-stricken area is in Western China, whereas the east, with its coastal ports, has the greatest industrialization under its Cancer/Capricorn MC/IC axis. China covers 9,615,767 square miles with a population of 1,367,330,000 in 2014.

Much of China falls under a Cancer Midheaven and a Libra Ascendant. Self-protectiveness and social cohesion are very evident in this vast country. It has had roughly 4,000 years of traditional national unity where long dynasties ruled the nation, and where, at the personal level, family tradition is honored, even worshipped. The Great Wall of China, which began construction in the third century BC, was built to protect the homeland from marauding invaders. In a country where the people are often crowded close together, they find peace and tranquillity for the soul by meditation, by their beautiful gardens, and by the love of their little birds that sing merrily from little bamboo cages hanging here and there.

Many countries fall under only one Midheaven and only one Ascendant. Japan, for instance, falls under the influence of a Leo Midheaven and a Scorpio Ascendant. Leo is exemplified in its title, The Land of the Rising Sun. It is said to have been founded by Jimmu Tenno, who was a direct descendant of the Sun Goddess. The Sun is the main feature of their national flag, red on a white background. The Japanese excel in sports and love entertainment, all Leo keywords. They are fiercely loyal to their Emperor, their families, and their employers.

The Scorpio Ascendant of Japan is vividly exemplified by their financial success. The Tokyo Stock Exchange is reputedly the most powerful money market in the world where trading is avidly pursued by the richest and poorest citizens alike, everyone vying for that Scorpio-based desire for unearned income or a slice of the country's industrial wealth. The political regime, from the top to the bottom, is openly controlled by big business; this is truly a land where wealth really matters. As an example, a golf club membership in a country club is big business, trading through various brokers for several million dollars. Consequently, many who love the sport never actually get to play on a golf course. They only experience the sport by hitting balls at a driving range, many of which are indoors.

Geodetic Country and City Rulerships

Observe the position of India on the Geodetic map. It has a Gemini Midheaven and a Virgo Ascendant, both ruled by Mercury. This is the country that produced writings in the oldest language in the world – Sanskrit. Nowhere is the diversity of Gemini more vividly displayed than in India with its vast number of states, provinces, kingdoms, tribal groups, and divisions of societies into economic, political, religious and ethnic groups.

The Western Atlantic coastline of Europe, with its Pisces Midheaven and Cancer Ascendant has more seaports than any other coastal area in the world. This was also where the greatest number of notable sea captains set sail from England, Spain, Portugal and France, to discover new lands to claim for their motherlands.

Iceland falls into the area of Pisces/Cancer and provides the world with the largest supply of cod fish, and the country has also given birth to many poets who write about romance, the sea, and spiritual matters.

Relating further to Pisces, move now to Mexico with its Pisces Ascendant and Sagittarius Midheaven. Mexico City was originally a Lake Village and much of its territory is made up of reclaimed swamp land and lake shore. It has one of the largest and most sumptuous cathedrals in the world and over sixty churches, as well as an exceptionally large number of jails. Both of these influences fall under the domain of Pisces.

To briefly and randomly point out a few cities, consider Athens with its Aries/Leo Midheaven/Ascendant, that was named after the Olympian Goddess Athena. It is the father of modern theatre and the home of the Olympic Games honoring physical fitness and sports prowess. Moscow with its Taurus/Leo Midheaven/Ascendant is the economic, cultural and social hub of Russia. The Leo Ascendant is clearly seen in any memorable visit to the Red Square in Central Moscow where the magnificently colorful St. Basil's Cathedral stands. The architecture of the many subway stations is unique, with ornate columns and high domed ceilings, some even adorned with chandeliers. It is like visiting a museum of art and history.

Russia has had considerable influence on world culture through its classical music, the ballet, and its architecture. The impressive Bolshoi theatre, established in 1773, houses one of the leading ballet and opera companies in the world. Mercer ranks Moscow as having the largest number of billionaire residents in the world and being the ninth most expensive city in the world.

Egypt, under Taurus/Leo, is the area of the great and enduring pyramids (Fixed Taurus) to bury and honour its kings (Fixed and kingly Leo), and the ageless Sphinx. The Sphinx is considered to be the greatest monumental sculpture surviving from the ancient world. The shape of the immense pyramids represent the rays of the Sun descending down to earth.

Shifting to cities on the North American continent:

Las Vegas, under the Sagittarius/Aquarius angles, is the gambling and divorce capital of the world.

Los Angeles, also under the Sagittarius/Aquarius angles, has highly publicized marital upheavals. It is the movie capital of the world, and a place where freedom of expression and life style seems magnified and freely expressed. It is also one of the most ethnically diverse cities in the United States under the influence of a Sagittarius Midheaven.

San Francisco, only a small geographic shift from Los Angeles, has quite a different flavour under the Scorpio/Aquarius Midheaven/Ascendant. It is the financial and commercial center of the west coast of the United States. After the devastation of the 1906 earthquake, it rebuilt itself in true transformative Scorpio style. It is also considered the gay capital of the United States.

Hartford, Connecticut, under Capricorn/Taurus, is a city proud of its many banks and is the home of many insurance company head offices. Connecticut was the first state to have the Constitution of the United States.

Detroit, Michigan, under Capricorn/Aries, houses the automobile industry. Mars rules mechanics and of course Capricorn is a sign of business and industrialization.

Edmonton, Canada, under the Geodetic angles of Sagittarius/Aquarius is a friendly city. Its modern City Hall built in 1992 was "designed as a people place, a place for civic government and a gathering place for Edmontonians", quoted from the city website and aptly reflecting its Aquarian Midheaven. At one time the city had the longest unused street car track in the world reflecting the principle of Jupiter expansiveness and optimism. The city was growing so rapidly that it outgrew the street car track before it could be used and bus transportation took over.

Many more examples could be developed but the above should be sufficient to prove the point that the characteristics of nations and cities respond to their Geodetic Equivalent angles. We will later deal with how they respond to the passing of transits, eclipses and multiple configurations.

For convenience the following pages list the cusps for major cities in the world with the longitude and latitude geographic coordinates. They have been computed from Solar Fire Gold V8 program, in the Placidus House Cusp system. As previously mentioned, Geodetic charts are special cusps with various charts inserted within, and a Geodetic map shows where the planets of any chart are angular.

Please note that Astro*Carto*Graphy also shows where the planets of any relocated chart are angular on a map of the world, making each chart individualistic. In other words, Astro*Carto*Graphy sets up a separate map for each chart, whereas the Geodetic concept has permanent zodiacal angles making it easy to see where planets of any chart fall in an angle anywhere in the world.

Both have validity, and in fact, I contributed a chapter comparing the two systems in *From Here to There: An Astrologer's Guide to Astromapping*, edited by Martin Davis, published by The Wessex Astrologer Ltd.

Similarities of Geodetic Co-ordinates with the Old Ptolemaic Rulerships

Many of the zodiacal signs, either by Midheaven or Ascendant of the Geodetic position, do correlate with the traditional country rulerships of Ptolemy's time, but for some of them a strong argument can be presented in favour of changes based upon their Geodetic reference. It would be too lengthy to name them all here, so only a few will be mentioned.

A considerable portion of Ptolemy's north-west quadrant which he called "fiery" in nature with a Midheaven of Aries, is also "fiery" in nature on the Geodetic map by either the Aries Midheaven or the Leo Ascendant, or both. Ptolemy gives Britain a fiery Aries nature. This fiery influence includes France, Germany and Denmark, which were also traditionally under the rulership of Aries.

Some authorities placed Russia under the rulership of Aquarius while others have suggested Taurus or even Sagittarius. We can understand the confusion when we observe the great variety of Geodetic Midheavens and Ascendants belonging to Russia.

There seems to be considerable discrepancy under the old Taurus rulership which includes Switzerland, Poland, Sweden and Ireland. We must agree, however, that Persia, now known as Iran, is placed here because geodetically it falls under the Taurus Midheaven area. We can now add the additional identification of its part-Leo and part-Virgo Ascendants.

The Geodetic rulerships do not correlate with any of the traditional Gemini countries except that Ptolemy indicates the outer regions of the north-east quadrant (see Figure #4) as being of the Air element. This reaches towards the Gemini Midheaven area on the Geodetic map. There is no correlation between Ptolemy's inner south-west Air Quadrant and the Geodetic Midheaven or Ascendant.

Traditionally such countries as Scotland, The Netherlands, parts of France and Africa are assigned to Cancer. Note that this is the Cancer Ascendant on the Geodetic map. Some authorities assign China to Cancer, while others feel Libra is more applicable. It is interesting to note on our Geodetic map that much of China has a Cancer Midheaven and a Libra Ascendant.

Leo has been assigned principally to France, Italy and Sicily. On the Geodetic map only a portion of Italy falls under a Leo influence by the Ascendant line.

The traditional Virgo countries generally include Greece, Babylonia, Mesopotamia, Turkey, sometimes Switzerland, more recently Brazil and the West Indies. In referring to the Geodetic map, we can only relate the Earth quality of the Taurus Midheaven to Turkey, and the Taurus Ascendant to Brazil.

There are no similarities between traditional rulers and the Geodetic divisions with Libra except the situation with China as mentioned above.

In connection with Scorpio, the only similarity that could be found was for Queensland, Australia, traditionally a Scorpio area which, on the Geodetic map, falls into a Scorpio Ascendant.

Under the sign of Sagittarius, the two systems have little in common, but in Charles E.O. Carter's *An Introduction to Political Astrology*, all of Australia is assigned to this sign. The Geodetic map shows the eastern half, which is the most densely populated portion, as having a Sagittarius Ascendant.

Capricorn's traditional rulership assignments have little relationship to the Geodetic divisions unless we stretch the relationship a little and consider some of the Earth element similarities. An example of this would be India which is traditionally ruled by Capricorn. Geodetically it has a Gemini Midheaven and an earthy Virgo Ascendant. Geodetically the Capricorn Midheaven encompasses Eastern Canada, Eastern United States and the north-west portion of South America, whereas the Capricorn Ascendant encompasses a portion of Western Canada, the Hawaiian Islands, Samoa, Fiji, etc. These are areas of which Ptolemy presumably had no knowledge.

Aquarius is in the same situation as Capricorn. Geodetically the Aquarius Midheaven of Greenland, Newfoundland and Brazil, and the Ascendant area of a portion of Canada and the United States, were areas beyond Ptolemy's geography.

Portugal and Normandy, traditionally assigned to Pisces, relate to the Geodetic Pisces Midheaven.

All of this, of course, is not enough to convince us to discard all the old rulerships and immediately replace them with Geodetic Equivalents, nor is it intended to do so. Only through accumulating evidence and continual research into the various potential applications can we find improved methods of technique and evaluation.

Geodetic Cusps
Major Cities in the United States

	MC	11th	12th	ASC	2nd	3rd
Anaheim **117W55 33N50**	02:05 Sag	24:51 Sag	17:53 Cap	16:33 Aqu	29:59 Pisc	05:19 Tau
Anchorage **149W55 61N10**	00:05 Sco	18:50 Sco	01:34 Sag	11:37 Sag	26:49 Cap	27:03 Pisc
Atlanta **84W23 33N46**	05:36 Cap	29:11 Cap	28:31 Aqu	09:21 Aries	16:17 Tau	12:51 Gem
Atlantic City **74W25 39N51**	15:34 Cap	09:20 Aqu	11:27 Pisc	27:47 Aries	00:50 Gem	24:18 Gem

Geodetic Country and City Rulerships

	MC	11th	12th	ASC	2nd	3rd
Berkeley 122W16 37N52	17:44 Sco	19:54 Sag	11:38 Cap	08:13 Aqu	23:37 Pisc	00:41 Tau
Boston 71W04 42N21	18:56 Cap	12:38 Aqu	16:01 Pisc	05:11 Tau	06:18 Gem	28:24 Gem
Boulder 105W16 40N01	14:43 Sag	05:50 Cap	29:12 Cap	02:23 Pisc	19:07 Aries	21:08 Tau
Burbank 118W18 34N11	01:41 Sag	24:24 Sag	17:20 Cap	15:49 Aqu	29:26 Pisc	04:54 Tau
Cape Canaveral 80W36 28N24	09:23 Cap	04:16 Aqu	04:49 Pisc	14:28 Aries	19:14 Tau	15:47 Gem
Chicago 87W39 41N51	02:20 Cap	23:51 Cap	21:19 Aqu	04:33 Aries	15:12 Tau	11:14 Gem
Cleveland 81W42 42N30	08:18 Cap	00:33 Aqu	00:04 Pisc	15:49 Aries	22:55 Tau	17:25 Gem
Coeur D'Alene 116W47 47N41	03:13 Sag	22:28 Sag	11:43 Cap	07:16 Aqu	01:53 Aries	09:05 Tau
Colorado Springs 104W49 38N50	15:10 Sag	06:34 Cap	00:18 Aqu	03:44 Pisc	19:33 Aries	21:25 Tau
Dallas 96W48 32N47	23:11 Sag	16:05 Cap	12:32 Aqu	18:50 Pisc	29:36 Ari	29:19 Tau
Detroit 83W03 42N20	06:57 Cap	28:50 Cap	27:47 Aqu	13:32 Tau	21:35 Tau	16:14 Gem
Fort Lauderdale 80W09 26N07	09:51 Cap	05:07 Aqu	05:50 Pisc	14:45 Aries	19:06 Tau	15:52 Gem
Fort Worth 97W19 32N44	22:40 Sag	15:33 Cap	11:54 Aqu	18:00 Pisc	28:53 Aries	28:44 Tau
Hartford 72W41 41N46	17:18 Cap	10:51 Aqu	13:37 Pisc	02:03 Tau	04:05 Gem	26:35 Gem

Geodetic Astrology for Relocating and World Affairs

	MC	11th	12th	ASC	2nd	3rd
Honolulu 157W52 21N18	22:08 Li	20:30 Sco	15:28 Sag	10:02 Cap	13:30 Aqu	19:01 Pisc
Houston 157W52 21N18	24:38 Sag	18:08 Cap	15:18 Aqu	21:33 Pisc	00:50 Tau	00:22 Gem
Kansas City 94W35 39N06	25:25 Sag	17:04 Cap	13:00 Aqu	21:37 Pisc	04:29 Tau	03:02 Gem
Las Vegas 115W08 36N10	04:51 Sag	27:01 Sag	19:50 Cap	19:07 Aqu	04:01 Aries	08:55 Tau
Los Angeles 118W15 34N03	01:45 Sag	24:29 Sag	17:27 Cap	15:59 Aqu	29:31 Pisc	04:58 Tau
Miami 80W12 25N46	09:48 Cap	05:07 Aqu	05:49 Pisc	14:37 Aries	18:56 Tau	15:46 Gem
New Orleans 90W04 29N57	29:55 Sag	23:42 Cap	21:58 Aqu	29:52 Pisc	07:50 Tau	06:07 Gem
New York 74W00 40N43	15:59 Cap	09:32 Aqu	11:48 Pisc	29:24 Aries	01:59 Gem	25:10 Gem
Palm Springs 116W33 33N50	03:27 Sag	26:09 Sag	19:20 Cap	18:25 Aqu	01:56 Aries	06:56 Tau
Pearl Harbour 157W56 21N21	22:03 Li	20:25 Sco	15:23 Sag	09:56 Cap	13:25 Aqu	18:54 Pisc
Phoenix 112W04 33N27	07:55 Sag	00:33 Cap	24:19 Cap	24:57 Aqu	08:16 Aries	12:06 Tau
Pittsburgh 80W00 40N26	10:00 Cap	02:43 Aqu	02:54 Pisc	18:34 Aries	24:33 Tau	18:54 Gem
Sacramento 121W30 38N35	28:30 Sco	20:28 Sag	12:05 Cap	08:45 Aqu	24:43 Pisc	01:42 Tau
Salt Lake City 111W53 40N46	08:06 Sag	29:06 Sag	21:12 Cap	21:07 Aqu	09:11 Aries	13:32 Tau
San Bernadino 117W18 34N07	02:41 Sag	25:22 Sag	18:25 Cap	17:13 Aqu	00:51 Aries	06:05 Tau

Geodetic Country and City Rulerships

	MC	11th	12th	ASC	2nd	3rd
San Diego 117W09 32N43	02:50 Sag	25:47 Sag	19:08 Cap	18:10 Aqu	01:03 Aries	06:04 Tau
San Francisco 122W25 37N47	27:35 Sco	19:47 Sag	11:32 Cap	08:05 Aqu	23:25 Pisc	00:28 Tau
Seattle 122W20 47N36	27:40 Scor	17:20 Sag	06:50 Cap	29:22 Cap	22:40 Pisc	02:09 Tau
Tempe 111W55 33N25	08:05 Sag	00:43 Cap	24:31 Cap	25:12 Aqu	08:30 Aries	12:17 Tau
Washington, DC 77W02 38N54	12:57 Cap	06:25 Aqu	07:41 Pisc	23:09 Ari	27:29 Tau	21:33 Gem

Geodetic Cusps
Major Cities of the World Excluding the United States

	MC	11th	12th	ASC	2nd	3rd
Adelaide Australia 138E35 34S55	18:35 Leo	19:08 Vir	28:07 Li	08:55 Sag	02:31 Cap	24:21 Cap
Algiers Algeria 03E03 36N47	03:03 Aries	08:53 Tau	16:09 Gem	18:54 Can	09:38 Leo	03:27 Vir
Amsterdam Netherlands 04E54 52N22	04:54 Aries	14:18 Tau	27:30 Gem	00:31 Leo	16:29 Leo	06:43 Vir
Ankara Turkey 32E52 39N56	02:52 Tau	08:53 Gem	13:14 Can	12:57 Leo	04:23 Vir	00:38 Li
Antwerp Belgium 04E25 51N13	04:25 Aries	13:24 Tau	26:07 Gem	29:18 Can	15:39 Leo	06:10 Vir
Athens Greece 23E43 37N58	23:43 Aries	29:40 Gem	04:39 Can	05:09 Leo	26:28 Leo	22:07 Vir
Auckland New Zealand 174E46 36S52	24:46 Vir	00:14 Sco	08:31 Sag	12:31 Cap	03:08 Aqu	26:13 Aqu
Baghdad Iraq 44E25 33N21	14:25 Tau	18:29 Gem	19:36 Can	19:38 Leo	13:10 Vir	11:52 Li

Geodetic Astrology for Relocating and World Affairs

	MC	11th	12th	ASC	2nd	3rd
Bangkok Thailand 100E31 13N45	10:31 Can	10:28 Leo	11:11 Vir	11:15 Li	11:19 Sco	11:06 Sag
Beijing China 116E25 39N55	26:24 Can	29:32 Leo	28:37 Vir	22:40 Li	20:26 Sco	22:07 Sag
Belfast Ireland 05W45 54N36	24:15 Pisc	02:59 Tau	20:08 Gem	25:30 Can	10:05 Leo	28:22 Leo
Berlin Germany 13E22 52N30	13:22 Aries	23:21 Tau	04:40 Can	06:07 Leo	22:33 Leo	13:48 Vir
Berne Switzerland 07E26 46N57	07:26 Aries	15:26 Tau	25:35 Gem	18:18 Can	16:15 Leo	08:14 Vir
Bogota Colombia 74W05 40N36	15:55 Cap	14:20 Aqu	15:50 Pisc	19:22 Aries	20:41 Tau	18:53 Gem
Brisbane Australia 153E02 27S28	03:02 Vir	05:51 Li	03:02 Sco	18:40 Sag	12:20 Cap	05:59 Aqu
Brussels Belgium 04E20 50N50	04:20 Aries	13:12 Tau	25:42 Gem	28:57 Can	15:26 Leo	06:03 Vir
Bucharest Romania 26E06 44N26	26:06 Aries	03:32 Gem	09:47 Can	10:01 Leo	29:48 Leo	14:28 Vir
Budapest Hungary 19E05 47N30	19:05 Aries	27:30 Tau	05:47 Can	06:44 Leo	25:09 Leo	18:21 Vir
Buenos Aires Argentina 58W27 34S36	01:33 Aqu	04:13 Pisc	03:26 Aries	28:12 Aries	26:42 Tau	28:09 Gem
Cairo Egypt 31E15 30N03	01:15 Tau	05:20 Gem	07:58 Can	07:44 Leo	01:22 Vir	29:06 Vir
Calcutta India 88E22 22N32	28:22 Gem	29:01 Can	29:23 Leo	28:21 Vir	27:14 Li	27:39 Sco
Calgary Canada 114W05 51N03	05:55 Sag	23:50 Sag	11:59 Cap	07:13 Aqu	06:49 Aries	13:19 Tau
Canton China 113E16 23N06	23:16 Can	24:44 Leo	25:15 Vir	22:59 Li	22:07 Sco	22:16 Sag

Geodetic Country and City Rulerships

	MC	11th	12th	ASC	2nd	3rd
Cape Town South Africa 18E22 33S55	18:22 Aries	15:34 Tau	08:20 Gem	29:59 Gem	05:43 Leo	14:18 Vir
Caracas Venezuela 66W56 10N30	23:03 Cap	21:37 Acu	24:07 Pisc	29:01 Aries	29:40 Tau	26:43 Gem
Copenhagen Denmark 12E35 55N40	12:34 Aries	23:52 Tau	06:56 Can	08:02 Leo	23:15 Leo	13:28 Li
Dublin Ireland 06W15 53N20	23:45 Pisc	02:03 Tau	18:21 Gem	23:58 Can	09:04 Leo	27:44 Leo
Edmonton Canada 113W28 53N38	06:31 Sag	23:23 Sag	10:20 Cap	04:12 Aqu	08:21 Aries	14:55 Tau
Gibraltar 05W21 36N08	24:39 Pisc	00:01 Tau	08:05 Gem	12:00 Can	02:48 Leo	26:02 Leo
Greenwich England 00W00 51N29	00:00 Aries	08:38 Tau	22:25 Gem	26:33 Can	12:36 Leo	02:33 Vir
Guatemala Guatemala 90W31 14N38	29:28 Sag	25:32 Cap	24:47 Aqu	29:18 Pisc	03:57 Tau	03:21 Gem
Halifax Canada 63W36 44N39	26:24 Cap	21:06 Acu	27:34 Pisc	18:58 Tau	15:53 Gem	06:14 Can
Havana Cuba 82W22 23N08	07:37 Cap	03:07 Acu	03:26 Pisc	11:04 Aries	15:37 Tau	13:06 Gem
Helsinki Finland 24E58 60N10	24:58 Aries	09:37 Gem	20:55 Can	18:53 Leo	03:26 Vir	24:01 Vir
Hong Kong China 114E09 22N17	24:09 Can	25:35 Leo	26:08 Vir	23:58 Li	23:09 Sco	23:15 Sag
Jakarta Indonesia 106E48 06S10	16:48 Can	15:08 Leo	16:46 Vir	20:40 Li	21:59 Sco	19:58 Sag
Jerusalem Israel 35E14 31N46	05:14 Tau	09:24 Gem	12:00 Can	11:36 Leo	5:08 Vir	02:56 Li

Geodetic Astrology for Relocating and World Affairs

	MC	11th	12th	ASC	2nd	3rd
Johannesburg South Africa 28E00 26S15	28:00 Aries	25:05 Tau	18:55 Gem	12:55 Can	18:23 Leo	25:18 Vir
Khartoum Sudan 32E32 15N36	02:31 Tau	04:21 Gem	04:32 Can	03:38 Leo	00:24 Vir	00:21 Li
Kiev Ukraine 30E31 50N26	00:31 Tau	09:46 Gem	16:53 Can	16:13 Leo	04:36 Vir	28:31 Vir
Kingston Jamaica 76W48 18N00	13:11 Cap	09:54 Aqu	11:17 Pisc	18:03 Aries	20:48 Tau	18:00 Gem
La Paz Bolivia 68W09 16S30	21:50 Cap	22:39 Aqu	23:35 Pisc	22:40 Aries	22:15 Tau	21:53 Gem
Llasa Tibet 91E09 29N40	01:09 Can	02:51 Leo	03:17 Vir	01:05 Lib	29:00 Li	29:27 Sco
Lima Peru 77W03 12S03	12:56 Cap	12:50 Aqu	13:42 Pisc	14:00 Tau	14:10 Tau	13:45 Gem
Lisbon Portugal 09W08 38N43	20:52 Pisc	26:15 Aries	05:37 Gem	10:35 Can	00:42 Leo	23:03 Leo
London England 00W10 51N30	29:50 Pisc	08:27 Tau	22:16 Gem	26:27 Can	12:30 Leo	02:24 Vir
Madrid Spain 03W41 40N24	26:19 Pisc	02:22 Tau	11:40 Gem	15:54 Can	05:32 Leo	27:58 Leo
Manila Philippines 122E00 14N35	01:00 Leo	02:10 Vir	03:15 Li	02:10 Sco	01:36 Sag	00:58 Cap
Mecca Saudi Arabia 39E49 21N27	09:48 Tau	11:59 Gem	12:39 Can	11:56 Leo	08:00 Vir	07:38 Li
Melbourne Australia 145E58 39S49	24:57 Leo	26:37 Vir	06:55 Sco	17:25 Sag	09:19 Cap	00:31 Aqu
Mexico City Mexico 99W09 19N24	20:50 Sag	15:54 Cap	13:31 Aqu	17:14 Pisc	24:04 Aries	24:42 Tau

Geodetic Country and City Rulerships

	MC	11th	12th	ASC	2nd	3rd
Montreal Canada 73W34 45N31	16:26 Cap	08:56 Aqu	11:23 Pisc	03:09 Tau	05:14 Gem	25:49 Gem
Moscow Russia 37E35 55N45	07:34 Tau	19:01 Gem	26:01 Can	23:44 Leo	11:05 Vir	04:41 Li
Munich Germany 22E34 48N08	11:34 Aries	20:03 Tau	29:55 Gem	01:57 Leo	19:44 Leo	11:53 Vir
Nanking China 118W47 32N03	28:46 Can	01:13 Vir	00:50 Li	26:22 Li	24:51 Sco	26:02 Sag
New Delhi India 77E12 28N26	17:11 Gem	18:48 Can	19:17 Leo	17:45 Vir	15:06 Li	15:27 Sco
Odessa Ukraine 30E44 46N28	00:44 Tau	08:36 Gem	14:42 Can	14:20 Leo	03:54 Vir	28:41 Vir
Oslo Norway 10E45 59N55	10:45 Aries	24:16 Tau	10:25 Can	10:35 Leo	23:56 Leo	12:30 Vir
Ottawa Canada 75W42 45N25	14:18 Cap	06:27 Aqu	08:00 Pisc	29:07 Aries	02:36 Gem	24:39 Gem
Panama City Panama 79W38 09N02	10:22 Cap	07:51 Aqu	08:46 Pisc	13:09 Aries	15:32 Tau	23:53 Gem
Paris France 02E20 48N52	02:20 Aries	10:30 Tau	22:25 Gem	26:06 Can	13:12 Leo	04:08 Vir
Prague Czech Republic 14E26 50N05	14:26 Aries	23:36 Tau	03:42 Can	05:11 Leo	22:30 Leo	14:30 Vir
Rangoon Burma 96E10 16N47	06:09 Can	06:17 Leo	06:48 Vir	06:28 Li	06:14 Sco	06:19 Sag
Rio de Janeiro Argentina 43W14 22S54	16:46 Aqu	18:56 Pisc	18:35 Aries	14:37 Tau	13:52 Gem	14:35 Can
Rome Italy 12E29 41N54	12:29 Aries	19:26 Tau	26:59 Gem	28:50 Can	18:30 Leo	12:11 Vir

Geodetic Astrology for Relocating and World Affairs

	MC	11th	12th	ASC	2nd	3rd
Saigon Vietnam 106E40 10N45	16:39 Can	16:38 Leo	17:42 Vir	18:07 Li	18:16 Sco	17:36 Sag
San Salvador El Salvador 89W12 13N42	00:48 Cap	27:03 Cap	26:32 Aqu	01:03 Aries	05:22 Tau	04:37 Gem
Santiago Chile 70W40 33S27	19:20 Cap	21:47 Aqu	21:42 Pisc	17:42 Aries	15:50 Tau	16:43 Gem
Seoul South Korea 126E57 37N32	06:57 Leo	09:50 Vir	08:20 Li	01:59 Sco	00:31 Sag	02:38 Cap
Singapore 103E51 01N16	13:51 Can	12:42 Leo	13:52 Vir	16:10 Li	17:15 Sco	16:04 Sag
Stockholm Sweden 18E03 59N20	18:03 Aries	01:47 Gem	15:03 Can	14:45 Leo	21:53 Leo	10:17 Vir
Sydney Australia 151E13 33S52	01:12 Vir	03:55 Li	12:57 Sco	20:42 Sag	13:02 Cap	05:19 Aqu
Taipei Taiwan 121E30 25N03	01:30 Leo	03:25 Vir	03:35 Li	00:20 Sco	29:24 Sco	29:51 Sag
Tangier Morocco 05W45 35N48	24:15 Pisc	29:33 Aries	07:33 Gem	11:29 Can	02:23 Leo	25:38 Leo
Tehran Iran 51E26 35N40	21:26 Tau	25:26 Gem	27:25 Can	26:08 Leo	20:05 Vir	18:41 Li
Tokyo Japan 139E46 35N12	19:46 Leo	22:17 Vir	20:56 Li	12:57 Sco	12:15 Sag	15:05 Cap
Toronto Canada 79W23 43N39	10:37 Cap	02:39 Aqu	02:49 Pisc	21:04 Aries	26:59 Tau	20:23 Gem
Tripoli Libya 13E11 32N54	13:11 Aries	18:28 Tau	23:38 Gem	24:43 Can	16:43 Leo	12:15 Vir
Vancouver Canada 123W07 49N16	26:53 Sco	16:05 Sag	14:08 Cap	26:15 Cap	21:08 Pisc	01:30 Tau

Geodetic Country and City Rulerships

	MC	11th	12th	ASC	2nd	3rd
Vienna **Austria 16E20 48N13**	16:20 Aries	24:57 Tau	03:58 Can	05:17 Leo	23:18 Leo	16:00 Vir
Warsaw **Poland 21E00 52N15**	21:00 Aries	01:05 Gem	10:38 Can	10:57 Leo	28:00 Leo	20:16 Vir
Wellington **New Zealand 174E47 41S18**	24:47 Vir	00:51 Sco	18:41 Sag	15:18 Cap	04:40 Aqu	26:45 Aqu
Winnipeg **Canada 97W09 49N53**	22:51 Sag	11:10 Cap	03:27 Aqu	12:46 Pisc	05:23 Tau	03:10 Gem
Yokohama **Japan 139E39 35N27**	19:39 Leo	22:09 Vir	19:52 Li	12:57 Sco	12:15 Sag	15:02 Cap

NOTE
Chart data computed on Solar Fire Gold V8 (2015)

CHAPTER 3

Relocational Geodetic Charts and Maps

A natal chart can be inserted into the Geodetic susps of any geographic location to determine its shift in resonance. This can easily be done manually or with the stroke of a key on any good computer program; it also applies to the natal Midheaven, Ascendant, and any other additions normally used. Progressions and transits can also be added to indicate developments.

Most astrology programs also produce individual Geodetic maps for any chart to see where planets are angular for impact. However, having a large wall map with the Midheaven and Ascendant lines drawn allows for quick assessment of planets from any chart. Eclipses and planetary shifts can be followed visually on such a map.

As previously mentioned, you can make your own Geodetic map from the coordinates given in Chapter 8. A wall map measuring 3'x5' can also be ordered directly from my website: www.astrologychrismcrae.com. The map has a particular drawback because it does not take intercepted signs into account nor does it show other houses planets could be posited in. Setting up the full range of cusps is more precise and detailed.

Your planets can also be transferred mathematically into longitudes, as follows:

For planets in signs ranging from Aries to Virgo inclusive, they would be East Longitude on a map starting at Greenwich in 30 degree intervals:

Change the number of complete signs into degrees at 30 degrees for each sign
+ Degrees and Minutes into next sign
= Geographic Longitude

Example: 16:42 Gemini
2 complete signs, 30 degrees each   = 60 Degrees
+ Distance into the next sign   16:42 Degrees
                                     = 76:42 East Geographic Longitude

On a map of the world this Midheaven line runs through the interior of Russia and India.

For planets in signs ranging from Libra to Pisces inclusive, they would be West Longitude on a map moving backwards from Greenwich in 30 degree intervals:

Example: 13:20 Capricorn
2 complete signs backward (Pisces and Aquarius) = 60 Degrees
+ degrees and minutes moving backwards   16:40 Degrees (29:60 – 13:20)
                                                =76:40 West Geographic Longitude

That line runs through Eastern Canada, Eastern United States, West Indies and South America.

Relocational Geodetic Charts and Maps

When travelling long distances, it is interesting to note subtle shifting circumstances and even a shift in attitude as we move across various time zones and Geodetic angles. On long overseas flights, the astute traveller can notice such subtle shifts. It is more noticeable when driving by car or travelling by train across continents in either an easterly or westerly direction. However, if you will be in one location for a while, it can be useful to create a whole Geodetic chart.

If you are planning to relocate your permanent residence, it is wise to set up the whole Geodetic cusps for that location. Everyone has some planets or aspects that would be easier or less overt if kept out of the angles, and other planets that it would be advantageous to highlight.

If changing residence, it may be important to consider the reason. I once had a client who was having a great deal of trouble concentrating on the completion of his Masters program. He was too easily distracted by social activities and other divergences and asked if a change of location would shift the emphasis. I recommended a move two time zones west that would put him in a more conducive environment. He shifted universities accordingly and completed his degree. Sometimes couples wish to be relocated together; that is much more complex.

As you travel, various planets shift houses. For instance, if natal Venus moves over the Geodetic Midheaven, you may make an important contact. As it passes over the Geodetic Ascendant you could meet someone who pleases you very much. If it moves into a Geodetic fifth house, you could fall in love.

Neptune, on the other hand, could correlate with confused travel and reservation arrangements, food or water contamination related upsets, or even a credit card theft, depending upon the house placement and aspects. With Neptune you could be deeply moved or inspired in that location and have a spiritual experience. If staying at a hotel, it would be wise to keep valuables in a hotel safe.

Mars over the ninth cusp can indicate confrontations with border officials. If it rules your ninth house natally, and it crosses the angle geodetically, the same or a similar event could occur.

Jupiter, of course, could bring fun, as well as problems related to over-indulgences or over-expenditures.

I once had a personal experience with Saturn on my Geodetic Midheaven. I had been on an extended lecture tour for over a month, speaking on many evenings, including weekend seminars. When I was not lecturing I was in transit. I had arrived at my last engagement late in the morning, trusting that I would be able to rest during the afternoon before my evening presentation. My Saturn/South Node in Sagittarius were on the Geodetic Midheaven of that location and rest was not mine to have. Directly from the airport I was whisked off to several radio stations and a television studio for interviews. Dinner was somewhat rushed before the evening presentation. The following day I also found myself agreeing to do an extra afternoon session before the evening presentation at the University, at which point I literally hung onto the podium to steady myself. Hence we can say that Saturn in a prominent Geodetic position can bring heavy responsibilities as well as achievement but it is important to cognitively understand what we commit ourselves to.

Planetary Influences

The following is a brief description of planetary influences as we move from one location to another. Naturally, aspects make a difference, as well as length of time spent in various locations:

The Sun Highlights vitality and self-confidence.
Can put one in an authoritative position.
Potential for meeting important or helpful people.
Assistance from those in authority.

The Moon Emotions and sensitivities are highlighted.
Under certain aspects could cause agitation or tears.
Under favorable aspects could feel "right at home".
May indicate a time of home-sickness.
May feel you have been there before as in a sense of déjà vu.

Mercury Exchanging ideas, communication.
Phoning home more often than usual.
Negotiating and/or signing documents.
Change of plans or arrangements.
Making a presentation.
Changing circumstances.

Venus Love, harmony, peace, pleasure.
Feelings of ease.
Attracting aura or influence.

Mars Energy, aggressive actions, confrontations, impatience.
Wanting to be "on the go" or stirring up some excitement.
Some conditions can bring accidents so caution is advised.

Jupiter Over-indulgence such as eating, spending, and gambling.
Carelessness.
Fun, feeling wonderful.
Expansion, honors, optimism.

Saturn May feel uncomfortable or restricted in the surroundings.
Surroundings could seem gloomy and austere.
If on a business trip, enhances seriousness and responsibility resulting in fulfilment.
Involvement or responsibility to an older person.

Relocational Geodetic Charts and Maps

Uranus Exhilarating, exciting.
Unexpected events of an unusual nature.
Great for the adventure seeker but could be unsettling for the more structured personality.

Neptune A degree of carelessness could cause disappointments and inconveniences such as misplaced luggage, stolen items, and confused reservations.
Beware of contaminated food, water, and be especially suspicious of seafood.
Eat only in respected restaurants and avoid fast food or street vendors selling snacks.
Can also be inspirational or may be thrilled by unusual beauty such as a very special tropical sunset.
Could have a spiritual experience.

Pluto Avoid getting involved with civil demonstrations or political dissension.
Be wary of dangerous terrain.
Do not get involved in complicated issues that are none of your business.
Avoid slum or questionable areas in a strange city.
If driving, avoid sparsely inhabited underground parking areas.

The following pages will present examples of Geodetic cusps with natal planets, secondary progressions and transits where applicable.

The first presentation includes the natal chart of John Fitzgerald Kennedy, 35th President of the United States. It is then transferred to the Geodetic cusps of Dallas, Texas where he was assassinated on Friday, November 22, 1963, at 12:30 PM CST. The transits, including eclipses and triggering New Moon are included.

The next presentation includes the natal chart of Lee Harvey Oswald, the man who assassinated John Fitzgerald Kennedy. It too is transferred to the Geodetic cusps of Dallas Texas including transits, eclipses and previous New Moon.
   Lee Harvey Oswald emigrated to Russia intending to stay, and then returned to the United States after two years with his Russian bride and baby. He entered Russia through Leningrad which has a Midheaven of 0° Taurus. Oswald's natal chart has the South Node of the Moon at 29° Aries conjunct Saturn at 28° Aries. His Sun, North Node, Venus, Fortuna and Mercury all hover on the fourth house. These planets are even closer to the IC of Moscow which was also highly influential in his life. Moscow has a Geodetic IC of 7:34 Scorpio.

Geodetic Astrology for Relocating and World Affairs

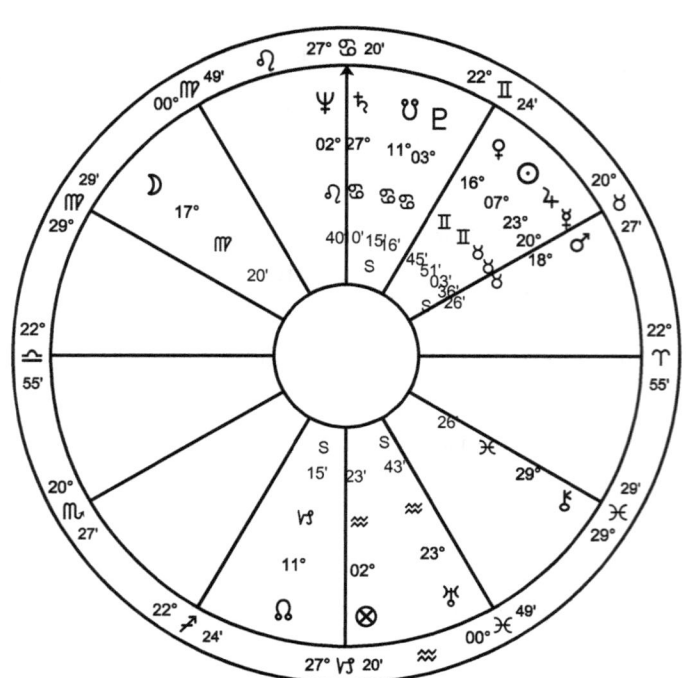

JOHN F. KENNEDY
Natal Chart
May 29, 1917, 3:15 PM
Brookline, Massachusetts
Tropical Placidus
Data: Rodden Rating A

INNER WHEEL: John F. Kennedy, GEODETIC CHART, Dallas, Texas
OUTER WHEEL: Transits November 22, 1963, 12:30 PM: Date of Assassination

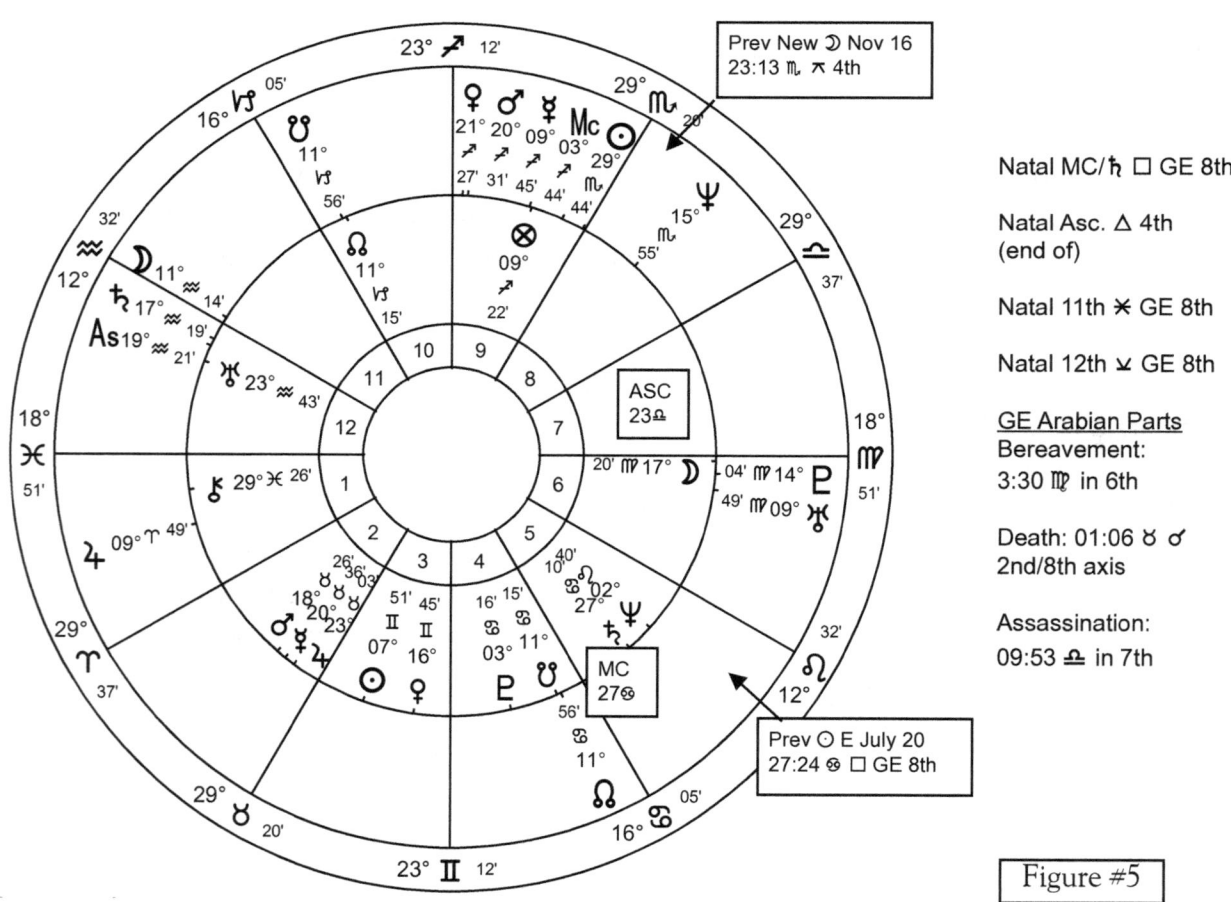

Natal MC/♄ □ GE 8th

Natal Asc. △ 4th
(end of)

Natal 11th ⚹ GE 8th

Natal 12th ⚺ GE 8th

<u>GE Arabian Parts</u>
Bereavement:
3:30 ♍ in 6th

Death: 01:06 ♉ ☌
2nd/8th axis

Assassination:
09:53 ♎ in 7th

Figure #5

Relocational Geodetic Charts and Maps

LEE HARVEY OSWALD
Natal Chart
Oct 18, 1939, 9:55 PM CST
New Orleans, Louisiana
Tropical Placidus
Data: Rodden Rating A

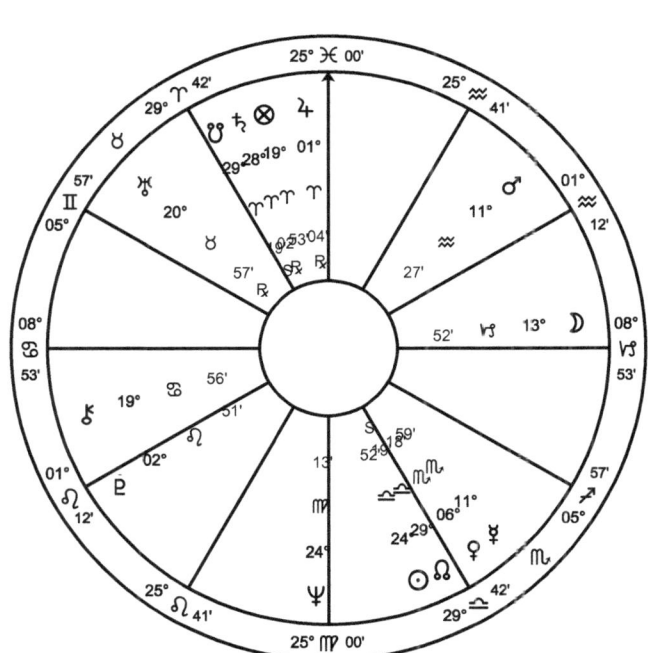

INNER WHEEL: Lee Harvey Oswald, GEODETIC CHART, Dallas, Texas
OUTER WHEEL: Transits November 22, 1963, 12:30 PM: Date of Assassination

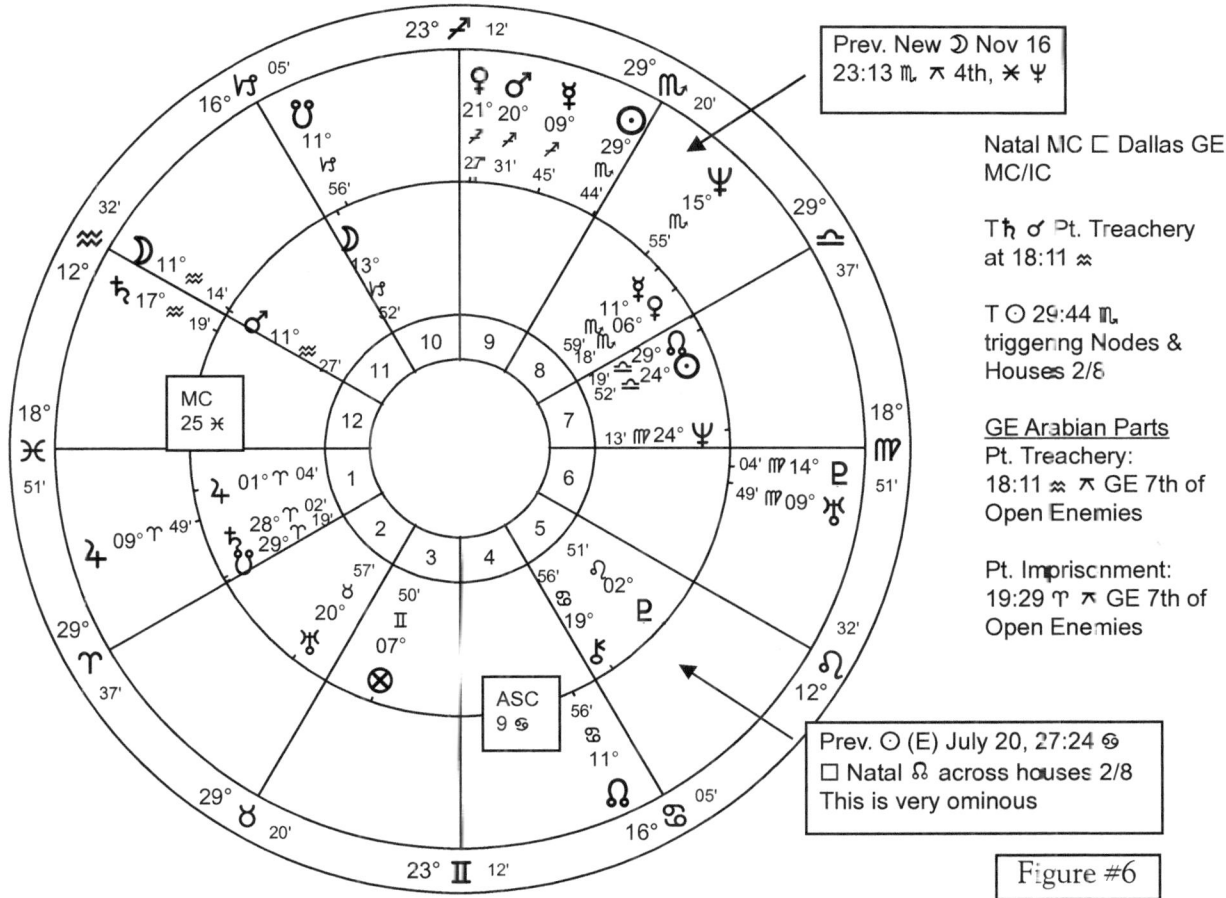

Figure #6

Application of the Geodetic Map

Sir Edmund Hillary

As previously indicated the Geodetic World Map shows the four permanent angles of the zodiac into which the planets of any chart can be added. (Refer to Figure #3.)

For this purpose we will use the chart of Sir Edmund Hillary, mountaineer, explorer, author and philanthropist (1919 –2008). He is accredited with being the first to reach the summit of Mount Everest with his fellow climber and guide, Tenzing Norgay. It is the tallest mountain in the world at 29,029 feet. As an adventurer Hillary travelled extensively for various significant reasons, which gives us an opportunity to observe the angular positions of applicable planetary influences on the Geodetic World Map.

As a philanthropist, he travelled widely to raise funds for the Himalayan Trust that he founded. With these funds

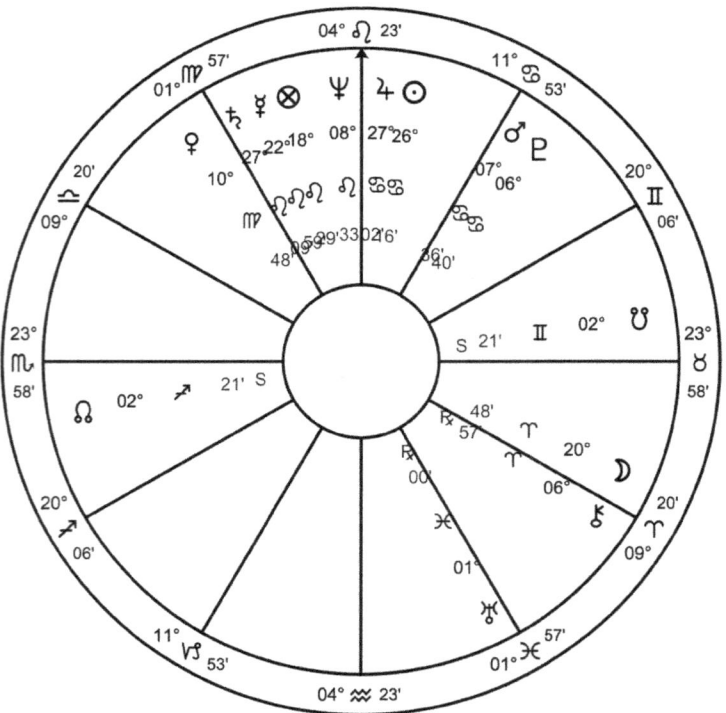

Figure #7 Sir Edmund Hillary Natal Chart
July 20, 1919, 12:30 PM, NZ –11:30 Papakura,
New Zealand Rodden Rating: DD

he built schools, hospitals, roadway systems, and an airport for flying in and out with greater ease and importing materials that changed the quality of life in the Himalayan region.

He was appointed High Commissioner of New Zealand to Nepal, as well as to India. For his many achievements, he was knighted by Queen Elizabeth II. His picture appeared on a New Zealand five dollar bill.

It would be helpful to first examine his natal chart before observing how his planets are positioned in the GE map. The time used here is somewhat speculative with a DD Rodden Rating, which means it is not supported by a birth certificate. Edmund Hillary's mother said he was born between 12:00 and 1:00 pm, hence the often used time of 12:30 pm.

In the natal chart we see areas that are strongly applicable to the public life of this man. First of all he was endowed with incredible physical power, energy and conviction, with his Mars/Pluto conjunction in Cancer in his eighth house. To scale a mountain like Everest takes enormous energy, stamina and physical fitness, overcoming oxygen deprivation and drawing on the mental demands of focus and strategy. Mars rules the sixth house of work, Pluto rules the determined, resourceful Scorpio Ascendant, and both are invigorated by a trine with uplifting Uranus ruling his fourth house of inner security daring to place his life in such a demanding position. His own purpose of life would have been energized by his passionate effort to change and uplift the life of the people he grew to love.

Relocational Geodetic Charts and Maps

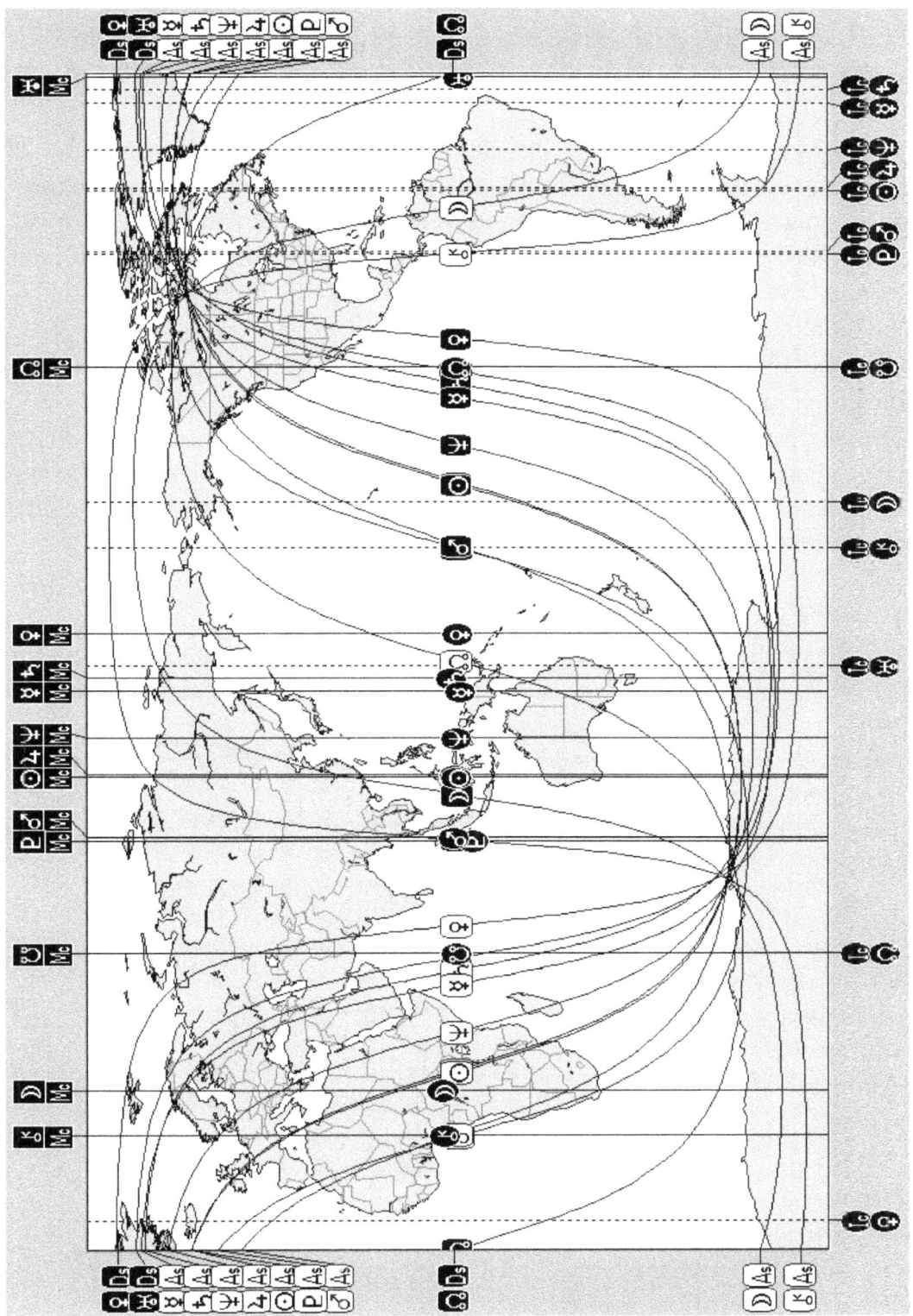

Figure #8 Geodetic Map for Sir Edmund Hillary
July 20, 1919, 12:30PM Papakura, NZ

The education he brought to the region correlates with the strong Mercury/Saturn conjunction in the tenth house; Mercury ruling schools and learning, and Saturn ruling the third house. The Sun/Jupiter conjunction in the ninth house correlates with his international recognition and the honor of knighthood bestowed upon him by Queen Elizabeth II.

We can observe how his natal planets are connected with the Geodetic map angles. The Geodetic Midheaven of this compulsive drive of transformative Mars/Pluto energy runs along the edge of Tibet very close to Mount Everest. This is where he made a second home for himself as he dedicated so much of his life and passion to improving the life of people in the region. The Sun/Jupiter Geodetic Ascendant runs through London, England, where he was knighted and where he raised funds to build schools and hospitals. His Venus Geodetic Ascendant line runs along the coastline of India where he was New Zealand's High Commissioner to that country as well as to Nepal and Bangladesh.

I also presented Sir Edmund Hillary's Chart and Geodetic Map in *From Here to There: An Astrologer's Guide to Astromapping*.

A separate chart could be made for each location Sir Edmund Hillary had strong connections with, but it is much more convenient to draw up a Geodetic map and observe where his significant planets are angular.

General George Patton

While watching the life of General George Patton in a movie called *Patton*, portrayed by George C. Scott, one becomes aware that he was a man of strong physical presence, controversial opinions and someone who, by his own confession, loved war. He was known for his unmitigated aggression and unrelenting discipline, ruling with an iron fist. This can be seen in the Mars apex T-Square pattern with the Mercury/Pluto opposition. Disruptive yet ingenious Uranus is also apex another T-Square with Venus and Saturn, suggesting the lack of tact and sensitivity. He was constantly in trouble with officials for his lack of discretion and for his statements that resulted in unsavoury press remarks. There is also a yod pattern with the Sun/Moon sextile going to his Ascendant.

He was a born strategist with the quintile triangle. Saturn and Mercury form a bi-quintile at 147:13 degrees from each other, each going to the North Node in Virgo in 5th harmonic quintile aspects. Astrologer Rick Levine calls this pattern a Golden Triangle due to its association with the 8-year

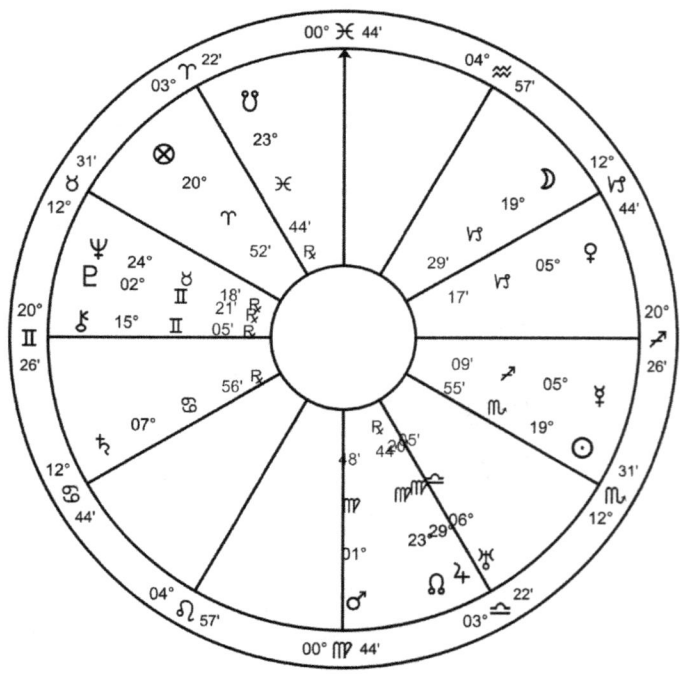

Figure #9 General George Patton Natal Chart
November 11, 1885, 6.38 PM, San Marino CA
Rodden Rating AA

Relocational Geodetic Charts and Maps

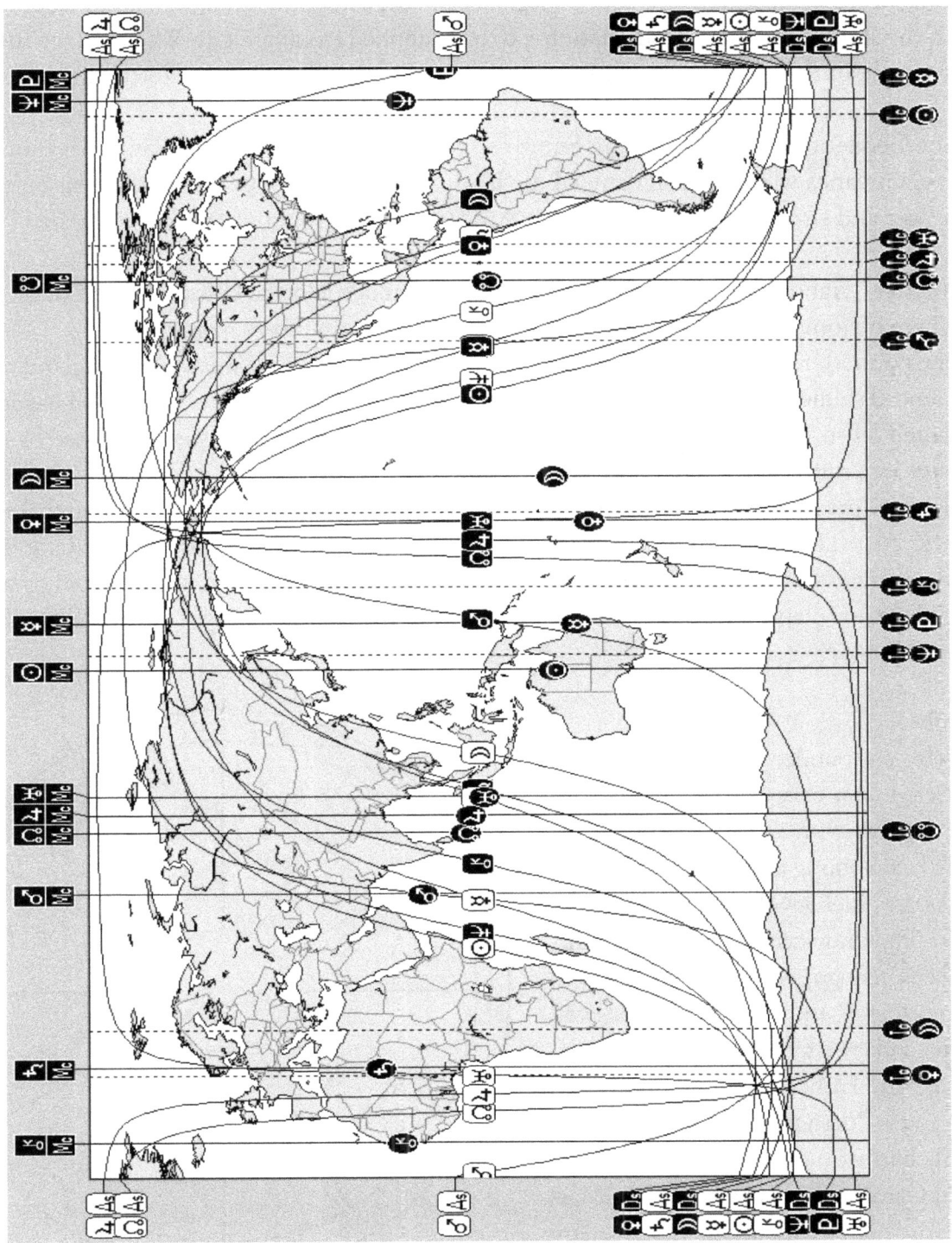

Figure #10 Geodetic Map for General George Patton
November 11, 1885, 6:38 PM, San Marino, CA

Quintile Star pattern and the Golden Mean measurements. Johannes Kepler referred to it as "magical". With Mercury being influenced in a magical formula with structural Saturn, we would associate this with the skillful and meticulous planning that he applied to campaigns. We can trace his military career throughout Europe where many lines cross, but his battle locations in North Africa were legendary.

On the Geodetic map, we can see his Saturn and Venus Ascendant/Descendant lines running right through Casablanca where he commanded the landing of 24,000 troops and won the siege, creating a military port and stronghold for other North African Campaigns. His opponents admired his genius even in defeat.

His Jupiter, Uranus, Moon Geodetic lines also run through North Africa and are not too far from Sicily where he joined both the American and British forces that were merging.

At one point, to remove him from public controversy in the field, he was sent to England to prepare inexperienced soldiers for a European campaign, and also to address various Women's Leagues. Those in command felt it would render him harmless but his outspoken manner was still noted by the press. His Jupiter line runs right through London.

His Jupiter line also runs through the beaches of Normandy where he landed just after the first initial attack. Allied Forces continued moving ever closer to Berlin, not too far from his Uranus line. In 1945 he asked for a command in the Pacific but was refused. This area is not influenced by any of his Geodetic lines or planetary angles. His main areas of influence have been the United States, North Africa and Europe.

Steve Jobs

Steve Jobs, co-founder and CEO of Apple Computers had a very interesting Geodetic map contact with China. Although he died much too young at the age of 56, he is known as the chief developer of the iPhone, iPad and iPod and according to Wikipedia, he has been recognized for his influence in both technology and music. He has been called "legendary, a futurist and a visionary", as well as "the Father of the Digital Revolution" and a "design perfectionist". From his natal chart we can observe that he has a powerful Cardinal Cross pattern with Mars in Aries in his eighth house (29°) square his brilliant Jupiter/Uranus conjunction in Cancer, square Venus in Capricorn. Neptune in Libra completes the Grand Square. The Nodes are also prominently featured in the axis of Cancer/Capricorn.

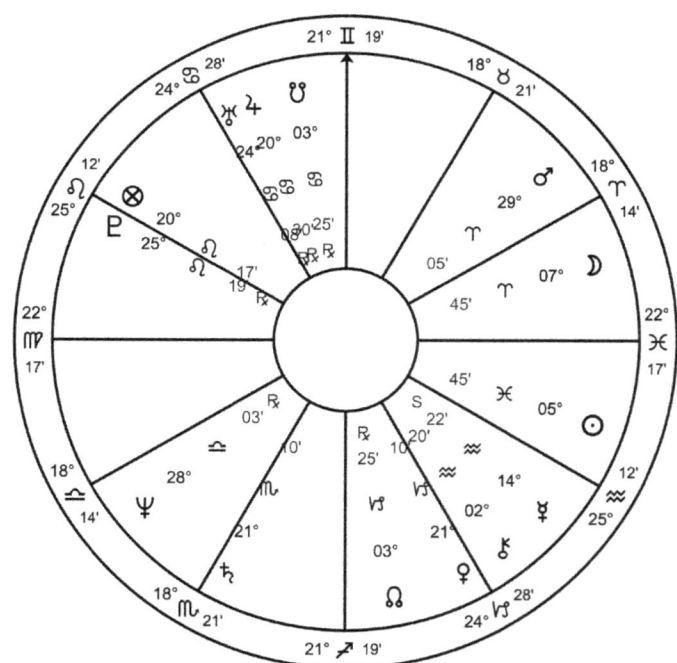

Figure #11 Steve Jobs Natal Chart
February 24, 1955, 7:15 PM, San Francisco, CA
Rodden Rating AA

Relocational Geodetic Charts and Maps

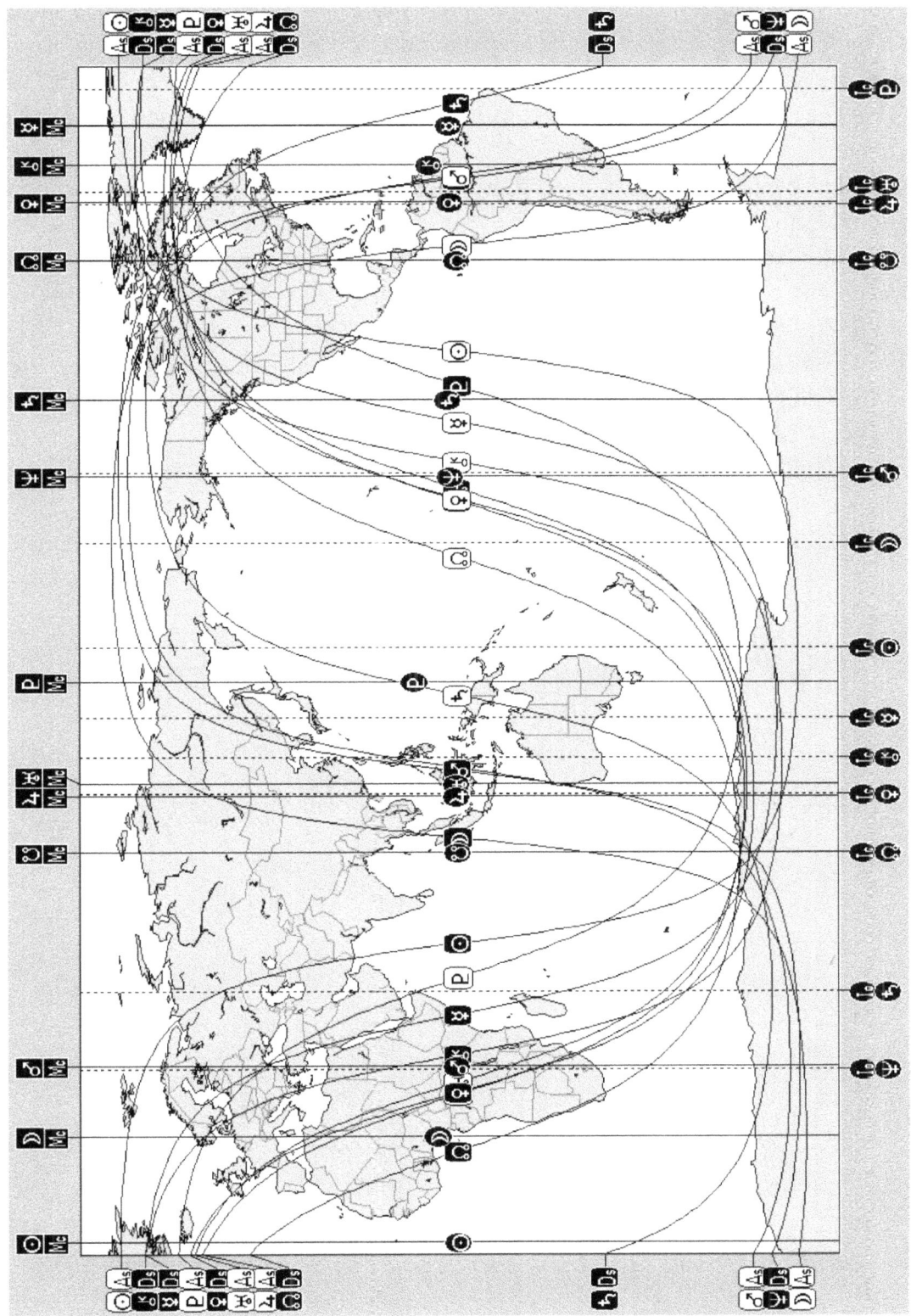

Figure #12 Geodetic Map for Steve Jobs

We will look at the Geodetic map on the previous page to see where these planets are angular to determine if he has a strong personal influence or connection in those areas. All the planets in the Grand Square are angular in China, either through the MC/IC axis or the Ascendant/Descendant axis. Note that they are primarily positioned in the eastern part of China which is the most densely populated, commercialized and industrialized area. Apple employs tens of thousands of Chinese factory workers, not only for its own company, but other subsidiary companies that produce components and material for production. The iPhone itself comes out of the factories in China, where the workers are over-worked, under-paid and tightly controlled. They are forced to live in dormitories with up to ten or twelve sleeping in a room. Meanwhile Apple itself is reported to have the largest bank account of any company in the world, allegedly in the range of billions.

The other significant Geodetic area for his natal chart is California where he was born, lived, created and died. His Pluto in Leo Ascendant runs through this area. It is in trine aspect with his Mars, linking both him and his company with China.

His Sun in early Pisces is also angular in the northwest corner of Mexico. It is possible that he had a vacation retreat somewhere in that area.

There are surely more geographic areas of interest but these are good examples of charts chosen at random.

CHAPTER 4

Geophysical Disruptions

From time immemorial, humanity has been deeply concerned with natural disasters, trying to predict when and where they will strike. These are events that are beyond its control and they are capable of unthinkable devastation of human life, massive economic loss and environmental shifts.

Earthquakes, volcanic eruptions, tidal waves, mud slides, and violent storms are among the most feared of natural phenomena. Prayers, incantations and sacrifices have failed to prevent the on-going menaces of nature. Modern science spends billions on research and equipment to shed some light on these phenomena but, with the exception of hurricanes and tidal waves, still cannot determine when and where many of these disruptive disasters will strike. Areas of probability for earthquakes and volcanic eruptions are known by the study of tectonic plates (see Figure #13 on page 41) and fault lines where cycles of occurrences are being studied.

It is not enough to ask why people live in areas of potential disaster. It would be easy enough to remove oneself from the locality of an active volcano but we also know that a volcano can remain inactive for centuries, lulling people into a sense of security, then it suddenly begins to stir, yawn, stretch, wake up and spew molten lava. It would be impractical to evacuate and keep uninhabited the vast global areas affected by both volcanoes and earthquakes as some of these regions provide food for the rest of the world. Devastating earthquakes and volcanic eruptions are relatively infrequent, whereas the frequency of smaller earthquakes is greater than most people realize. More will be discussed on this subject under the heading of Earthquakes.

As astrologers, we join these battalions of researchers because we understand that all life on our planet is affected by the predictable movement of the stellar bodies. What happens "up there" has a definitive effect "down here". The effect of planetary energy upon our human psyche affects our behavioral patterns and, if this has any credibility, it stands to reason that this energy must also affect our atmosphere as well as the planet itself.

However, we need to support our astrology with the latest scientific research so that we remain aware of the areas of greatest weakness. A solid rock foundation such as the vast Canadian Shield, for example, is unlikely to break at the onslaught of such elemental forces so we can turn our attention to areas of the world that are more likely to rumble and heave, or suffer with vicious winds, or crack and spew up boiling lava. Perhaps the time will come when astrologers and seismologists can work together so that we can have sufficient advance warning to at least minimize the loss of human life.

It is appropriate to digress somewhat in order to make a comparison of astrological influence on geography with its influence in our personal lives. When we are young adults we are dealing basically with personality thrust and with building the foundation of our lives. It is a trial and error method with many flaws and weaknesses, when we are prone to changes, losses and devastation as we respond to the cosmic pressures bearing down upon us. As we mature and gain a greater understanding of ourselves, the world around us, and the personal world we are creating, the less likely we are to be ripped apart by the cosmic flow. Not even Uranus or Pluto transiting the seventh house with adverse aspects can destroy a relationship that is working well, nor can adverse Saturn aspects destroy a career and reputation if it has been built on a solid foundation. Certainly these transits will likely indicate important adjustments but they need not be destructive. In other words, it is a question of strength versus the degree of weakness, in both the personal and the geophysical.

In terms of solidity and shifts on the surface of our planet, a strong cyclic influence over a given area will not necessarily erupt down the entire fault line but will choose the weakest part with perhaps only a minor adjustment required, like a small earthquake, or the spewing of steam or gas from a volcano. Then again, no shift or eruption occurs where the tectonic plate is solid, at least not during a certain period of geological time. If we are to be successful in predicting these types of disasters, we need to keep abreast of pertinent geological and seismological knowledge and discoveries. In the same way, if we are to make political predictions, we need to know the current conditions that exist.

One of the biggest problems we face in our dilemma of predicting geophysical disruption is in knowing where weakness lies. Equally, as we watch over the kaleidoscope of cyclic movement in the heavens, we need awareness of where the greatest area of vulnerability exists. Working with seismologists would of course be the best option, but in the meantime we should apply the highly significant knowledge we have and continue to accumulate our own evidence.

The object of this book is to share observations made from accumulating evidence over many years of study. There is much to support the Geodetic Equivalent concept as a viable frame of reference, not only in predicting disasters but also political upheavals and shifts in societal consciousness. The intention is to examine past phenomena carefully, observe re-occurring principles, then make applications into the future. However, there is much yet to learn.

Mundane Astrology

The astrology of world events is called mundane astrology. It covers geophysical disruptions, devastating storms, political activity, as well as the unfoldment and evolutionary process of mankind itself.

Over time, several different methods or frames of reference have been developed with varying uses and levels of success; I have listed several below, but I would heartily recommend reading *Mundane Astrology, An Introduction to the Astrology of Nations and Groups* by Michael Baigent, Nicholas Campion, and Charles Harvey.

1. Quarterly Ingress charts: These can be set for Greenwich and relocated to any other geographic location.

An ingress chart is set for the moment when the Sun enters 0 degrees of each cardinal sign, Aries, Cancer, Libra, and Capricorn, marking the start of the four seasons. These charts are limited in their predictive ability perhaps because of their general nature and time frame over a three-month period when other planetary influences can form.

2. National Horoscope coupled with the chart of its leader: This method is useful when concentrating on one particular country. However, it becomes more complex when trying to locate where a powerful planetary event in the sky will manifest on earth, so a search of many charts may be necessary. Computers and a list of world horoscopes can facilitate this greatly. A comprehensive list compiled by Nicholas Campion is available through astrolabe.com and also in his book, *The Book of World Horoscopes*.

3. The Study of Cycles: The most important astrological cycles combine two or more of the outer planets. These so-called Great Conjunctions have varying time spans of unfoldment from a Neptune/Pluto conjunction of over 492 years, to a Mars/Pluto conjunction of approximately 687 days. This is a complex study because there are many cycles functioning within other cycles, each going through phases of waxing and waning similar to the pattern of lunar phases and their meanings as laid out by Dane Rudhyar. Each cycle has a beginning, a stage of development, a coming to illumination or fruition, then a disseminating and concluding phase, only to start again at another level. Small cycles work within the context of the larger ones; they also work within each one of us individually in a microcosmic way and on the world stage macrocosmically.

4. Astro*Carto*Graphy®: A map is drawn of a particular astrological configuration such as a lunation, an eclipse, or a Great Conjunction etc., to determine where in the world it will be angular. It is known that angular planetary positions command greater attention and activity than succedent or cadent positions. Astro*Carto*Graphy®, developed by Jim Lewis in the mid 1970s, has become a popular framework for the judgment of events. Usually a separate map must be drawn for each planetary influence.

5. Lunations and Eclipses: These charts can be set for Greenwich and then relocated to any city, town, or country. Lunations are interpreted as the triggers for events that may have been foreshadowed by eclipses or Great Conjunctions.

6. Geodetic Equivalent Chart and Map: The Geodetic map shows where any planet or eclipse degree can be observed in its angular position, because the four angles are permanently preset on a map of the world. A quick glance at this can be useful in determining the potentiality of an event, or it can be shown in a full chart version for more detail. It is a framework for mundane astrology worthy of application and further research, as in the many examples that follow in this book.

The approach to successful mundane predictions is to find a viable frame of reference, examine past phenomena carefully, list reoccurring principles, then apply it to the future.

Firstly, it is useful to analyze the actual astrological event such as an eclipse, lunation, or Great Conjunction in an Aries chart to determine its full potential. This is often set initially for Greenwich. It is then easy to locate where the angular position of those degrees will be on a Geodetic World Map. Even without the map, the Midheavens are easy to ascertain, though not the location of the Ascendant/Descendant angles. Experience indicates that the influences falling across all four angles are indicators of events. Good astrology programs will do this work for us by relocating any chart to its exact geodetic angles, either in a chart or on a map.

Earthquakes

We know that earthquakes, as frightening as they can be, are only a small part of the geological changes occurring constantly on the earth. It is often not realized that out of the ongoing frequency with which they occur (over 500,000 each year), only about 100,000 can actually be felt. Some are so small we don't notice them, and many occur beneath the ocean floor.

Tsunamis

The larger oceanic disruptions create tidal waves called tsunamis, such as periodically strike the coastline of the Hawaiian Islands and Japan. Tsunamis are not so prevalent in California, although there was one in 1812 which created waves as high as 15 meters (50 feet) that hit the Santa Barbara coast.

The Great Chilean Earthquake of May 22, 1960, magnitude 9.5, created huge tsunami waves that measured 25 meters (82 feet) high, causing extensive damage throughout the Pacific Ocean, especially Australia, New Zealand, the Hawaiian Islands, Japan, and up the west coast of North American to Alaska. Giant waves up to 10.7 meters (35 feet) swept through the city of Hilo on the Big Island of Hawaii, reaching far inland and destroying much of the city. Tsunami waves travel up to 500 miles per hour and were able to reach the Hawaiian Islands about fifteen hours after the eruption. (See Figure #16.)

The massive tsunami on December 26, 2004, hit shore lines throughout Indonesia, India and Africa, and was measurable as far away as the coasts of North and South America. (See Figure #21.)

A list of historical as well as more recent tsunamis and earthquakes can easily be found online.

Earthquake Zones and Theories

We need not be overly concerned with the scientific causes of earthquakes, nor is it my area of expertise, however, a little background may prove both useful and interesting.

There are two broad belts where most of the serious quakes occur. The first is the Pacific Fire Circle, which ranges up the west coast of South America, northward along California, up to Alaska and through the Aleutian Islands, proceeding south past Japan, the Philippines and the East Indies. This can be observed in Figure #13 as the Pacific Tectonic Plate. The other main seismic zone extends through the Mediterranean Sea eastward through Turkey and on through China to join the Pacific Fire Circle around the region of the East Indies. This can also be seen on the same map as the lower region of the huge Eurasian Plate.

As we can see, the earth's crust is irregularly divided into divisions called tectonic plates, there being about seven or eight large ones and several smaller ones like the Nazca Plate off the coast of Chile, and an even smaller one off the coast of British Columbia and Washington State called the Juan de Fuca Plate. These are also marked in Figure #13.

Many scientists support the continental drift theory that the earth's land area was once a large mass that broke into pieces and began drifting. Along the edge of these plates or faults there are weaknesses creating fissures that are smaller faults. These weaknesses are caused by the grinding of plates together

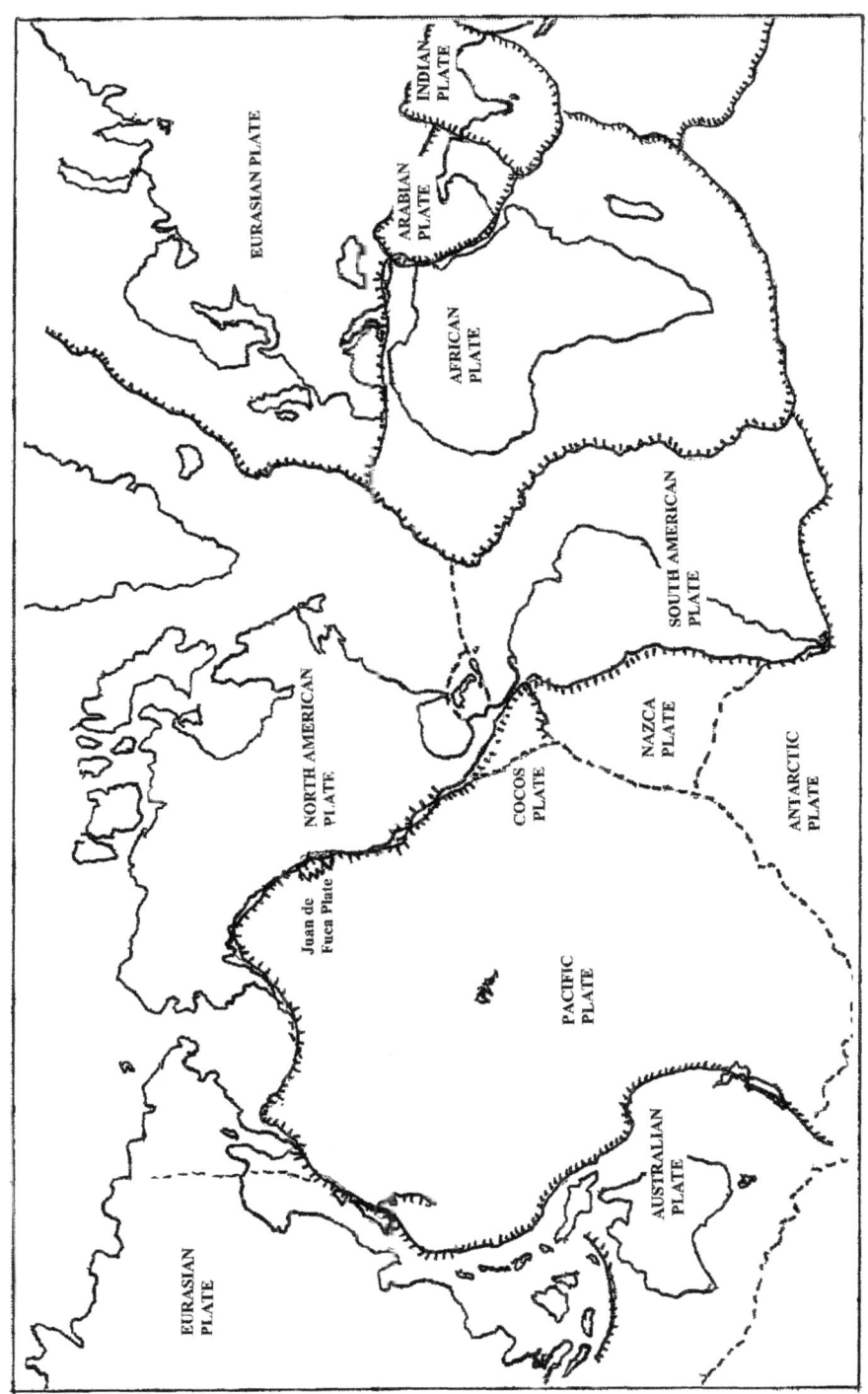

Figure #13 Tectonic Plates
Approximated from *The London Times Atlas of the World*, 1978 Edition. There appear to be about 7 main plates with a few subsidiary plates. Not all boundaries are certain.

as they are forced against one another, often moving in opposite directions. One of the sources of this grinding pressure comes from the high ridges along the ocean floor, from below which hot molten lava oozes, solidifies, and pushes the crust outward while other plate edges, at the same time, are being shoved downward, where they melt and continue the cycle. An example of this activity is the Nazca Plate off the west coast of South America, which is being forced into a deep trough and is thus pushing up the Andes Mountain range causing Great Earthquakes and tsunamis.

The problem in California is thought to be caused by the Pacific Plate, which gets stuck as it moves in a north-westerly direction towards the Aleutian Islands, then pressure, presumably from below, pushes with such force that the ground ripples and buckles. This is the region of the San Andreas Fault. It is not the only fault or fissure in California but it is by far the most well known. There are literally hundreds of faults but only certain ones are notable by reason of their activity during the period of record keeping. They are all, however, believed to belong to the same system of San Andreas.

A similar complex process seems to exist between the African, Eurasian and Arabian Plates, in creating the Anatolian Fault, comparable to the San Andreas Fault. This Anatolian fault produces a noticeable number of Great Quakes ranging between 7 to 8+ on the Richter scale.

The very small oceanic plate called the Juan de Fuca Plate, previously mentioned, is presently locked under the edge of the large North American Plate. It includes a portion of the coastline of British Columbia, all of the State of Washington, and down to about Medicino in Northern California where it seems to intersect the San Andreas fault.

Seismologists in both Canada and the State of Washington report that a megathrust earthquake in this area is long overdue, indicating that it springs free approximately every 300–600 years. It is estimated that the last one occurred about the year 1700. According to carbon dating of residue, that particular quake would have reached a magnitude of somewhere between 8.7 and 9.2, creating tidal waves that would have devastated the entire coastline.

Some geologists are of the opinion that earthquakes are the result of thermal contraction. This basically means that, as the earth cools from its molten state, it creates a wrinkling and cracking effect.

Then there is the convection theory that suggests that portions of the crust are dragged down towards the molten core, which then squeezes rock upwards, creating mountains. Either of these theories could explain the earthquake activity in an area such as Yellowstone National Park, mostly situated in the state of Wyoming but stretching into Montana and Idaho. This is an area of extensive buckling and fracturing. Then one must wonder what caused the massive earthquakes in 1811–12 around New Madrid, Missouri, along 90° West Longitude, measuring as high as 8.0 on the Richter scale. There is still much to learn.

The Richter Scale of Measurement
The Richter scale has been the standard of measurement since 1935. Intensity is measured in both whole numbers and fractions. For every whole number, there is a tenfold increase in the size of the quake record, so an earthquake of 5.0 creates a shock wave that is ten times greater than an earthquake registering 4.0, and releases energy that is 31.6 times more than released by the smaller quake.

An earthquake that reaches a magnitude of 7+ on the Richter scale is called a Major Earthquake. A 6+ magnitude is generally considered moderately destructive but in a densely populated area the destruction is much greater. A magnitude of 4.5 is considered slight, being felt only about twenty miles from its epicentre. Anything under that is barely felt, except that it can be registered on seismic instruments. The term 'Great Earthquake' is applied to intensities of 8+, such as the famous San Francisco quake of 1906 which reached 8.3, and the Great Chilean Earthquake of 1960 as mentioned above. Some of these will be chosen as chart examples of high intensity planetary energy that influences a particular area seeking out the weakest spot. Even though an earthquake of 5.0–5.5 is considered small, creating little damage, I am told its effect on the human psyche is very shocking. Firstly, a person caught at the beginning of an earthquake does not know how long it is going to last, and secondly, terra firma that normally feels so secure, begins quivering like a bowl of jelly and there is no place to run even if your knees would function. First hand accounts of even small quakes tend to be somewhat inflated adding more fright for the novice.

The intention here is to put it all in perspective. We will discuss and examine the historically monumental quakes, not with the intention of frightening anyone but because the larger ones provide greater scope for study. This can give us the most useful information to determine when and where a Major or Great Earthquake will occur, so that ultimately we might reduce the number of lives taken and the staggering costs of repair. A list of guidelines in making such predictions will follow in Chapter 7.

Eclipses in Forecasting Earthquakes

In determining if an area is earmarked for a special event, the most important astrological information can be obtained from solar eclipses. There are two eclipse seasons a year with the eclipses most often in opposite signs, and accompanied by either a North or South Lunar Node, creating what can be termed an eclipse axis. The possibility of an event happening is increased when these solar eclipses occur within an orb of ten degrees in opposition to each other and falling across a Geodetic map angle or in an angular house of a chart.

Once the eclipse is fully evaluated by setting up its chart, the pertinent signs and degrees can be set on a Geodetic map framework to see where they are angular and thus indicate the potentiality of an event. If this is in a highly active seismic area of the world, a forecast or prediction can therefore be made.

For this work you will need a list of eclipses. An ephemeris lists them for the month, day and GMT time they occur, but a separate eclipse list will certainly make your life easier. An excellent source is *Tables of Planetary Phenomena*, by Neil F. Michelson, in which eclipses are listed from 1700 to 2050. These tables show both solar and lunar eclipses, dates and times, as well as the Greenwich Mean Time so you can calculate the whole chart, eclipse description, and astrological position.

The Eagle and the Lark by Bernadette Brady lists the solar and lunar Eclipses from 1900 to 2050, as compiled using Michelsen's *American Ephemeris for 20th Century*.

All eclipses belong to a particular family group called a Saros Series. It is a convenient system of organizing a series of eclipses over a period of time that share similar geometry and similar characteristics. An eclipse in the same family will occur every 18 years + 10/11 days, over a period of about 1200–1300 years resulting in 70 or more eclipses.

An eclipse series will begin either at the north or south pole with several short partial eclipses, working its way in the same direction further north or south depending on its starting point. Partial eclipses become annular eclipses, then become hybrid eclipses (part annular and part total), until they graduate to a total eclipse affecting the central region of planet earth. The procedure then reverses until that particular cycle drops off the planet at the opposite pole from where it started. At the present time of writing, in 2015, there are about 39 different Saros Series running. A montage of every solar eclipse path over a twenty-year period would look like a mass of disorderly lines, whereas in fact it is totally systematic with many series running concurrently.

There are two different Saros Series numbering systems. The Brady book uses a system of numbering from 1–38, South and North, Old and New. The same numbering system is used by Robert Carl Jansky in *Interpreting Eclipses.*

The numbering system that we are using here was developed by G. Van de-Bergh in 1955 and is used for numbering eclipses on the NASA website. It is also a popular system with many astrologers. The numerical sequence listed on the NASA website starts at Saros #1, June 4, –2872. The various Saros Series now running range from the oldest #117, which started in the year 0792 and will end in 2054, to the newest #156 that started on July 1, 2011 and will end in 3237. As one cycle ends another begins.

The even Saros numbers are South Nodal, near the Moon's descending node, where the shadow is moving on earth in a west-north direction. The uneven Saros numbers are North Nodal eclipses near the Moon's ascending Node, where the shadow is moving in a west-south direction.

Let us isolate a ten-year block of solar eclipses and briefly examine the patterns. Partial eclipses do not have a period of duration. They are indicated by magnitude, or "fraction of the Sun's diameter obscured at greatest eclipse" as explained on the NASA website. Notice the small percentage of obscurity for Saros #117 in 2018 because it is very close to the end of its long cycle.

Year	Date	Type	Duration/Magnitude	Position	Saros
2017	Feb 26	Annular	Max. Duration: 0 min 44 sec	08:12 Pisces	Saros #140
	Aug 21	Total	Max. Duration: 2 min 40 sec	28:53 Leo	Saros #145
2018	Feb 15	Partial	Magnitude: 0.599	27:07 Aquarius	Saros #150
	July 13	Partial	Magnitude: 0.337	20:42 Cancer	Saros #117
	Aug 11	Partial	Magnitude: 0.737	18:41 Leo	Saros #155
2019	Jan 6	Partial	Magnitude: 0.715	15:26 Capricorn	Saros #122
	July 2	Total	Max. Duration: 4 min 33 sec	10:38 Cancer	Saros #127
	Dec 26	Annular	Max. Duration: 3 min 39 sec	04:07 Capricorn	Saros #132
2020	June 21	Annular	Max. Duration: 0 min 38 sec	00:21 Cancer	Saros #137
	Dec 14	Total	Max. Duration: 2 min 10 sec	23:08 Sagittarius	Saros #142
2021	June 10	Annular	Max. Duration: 3 min 51 sec	19:47 Gemini	Saros #147
	Dec 4	Total	Max. Duration: 1 min 55 sec	12:22 Sagittarius	Saros #152

2022	Apr 30	Partial	Magnitude 0.640	10:29 Taurus	Saros #119
	Oct 25	Partial	Magnitude 0.862	02:01 Scorpio	Saros #124
2023	Apr 20	Annular	Max. Duration 1 min 16 sec	29:50 Aries	Saros #129
	Oct 14	Annular	Max. Duration 5 min 17 sec	21:08 Libra	Saros #134

There are several features to notice from the list:

There are only two eclipse seasons every year, a little less than six months apart.

Most eclipse seasons have only one pair that occur in opposite signs and Nodes, with few exceptions. However, note that in 2018 there are three solar eclipses that are not partials.

Note in the summer eclipse season of 2018 that two solar eclipses occur approximately one month apart. If we go back 18 years and 11 days to the year 2000 we see Saros #117 and #155 within thirty days of each other. This occurs occasionally because of the 18+ year repetitive factor of eclipses in the same series.

The reason for this occasional occurrence is because a new series begins as an old one finishes and sometimes this overlap occurs.

They move in backward motion through the zodiac.

One can use the sign and degree of the eclipse axis for a quick scan on the Geodetic map to find the most vulnerable area for an event, in this case an earthquake if it is in a volatile seismic area. We know that angular positions are the most vulnerable as we will see by examples given in the following pages. Remember that we are considering an eclipse pair that is less than ten degrees apart, as well as considering its duration, to determine the amount of energy or pressure being applied in a given area.

On the subject of duration, we are alerted to any solar eclipse that lasts over three or four minutes. The longest eclipse on record occurred on December 14, 1955 at 21:31 Sagittarius. It lasted 12 minutes 09 seconds. Following this was the eclipse of December 24, 1973 at 12 minutes 02 seconds. The next longest were two eclipses both over 11 minutes, one in 1919 and the other in 1901. I wondered why the four longest eclipses on record all occurred in the twentieth century, and curiosity prompted me to look at the first fifteen years of the twenty-first century, where I found seven solar eclipses with a duration of 5 minutes or longer. This information is listed in *Tables of Planetary Phenomena*.

Observing only the eclipse axis is useful for a quick scan but not sufficient for more detailed and accurate work. For this we need the whole eclipse chart, which makes it easier to see what other influences exist. Is there a planet conjunct, in opposition or square the eclipse degree? We can put the eclipse chart on the inside of the geodetic cusps for a chosen region and watch the transits and lunations over the following six months, at which time another eclipse pattern has developed. It is like a moving mini ephemeris. I like to keep a binder with a record of eclipse charts over a period of several years.

Eclipse charts are easy to calculate from data contained in most good astrological programs or from the GMT that is listed with an eclipse list. The Kepler software program draws the eclipse path on a map. Several can be drawn on the same map and it is interesting to see how they appear to be scattered across the globe, but there is a very profound and exact system in operation. On the following map (Figure #14) we can observe all solar eclipses for a period of five years, from 2017 to 2022. Some are total or annular, while some are partial, being closer to either the north or south pole where they enter the cycle.

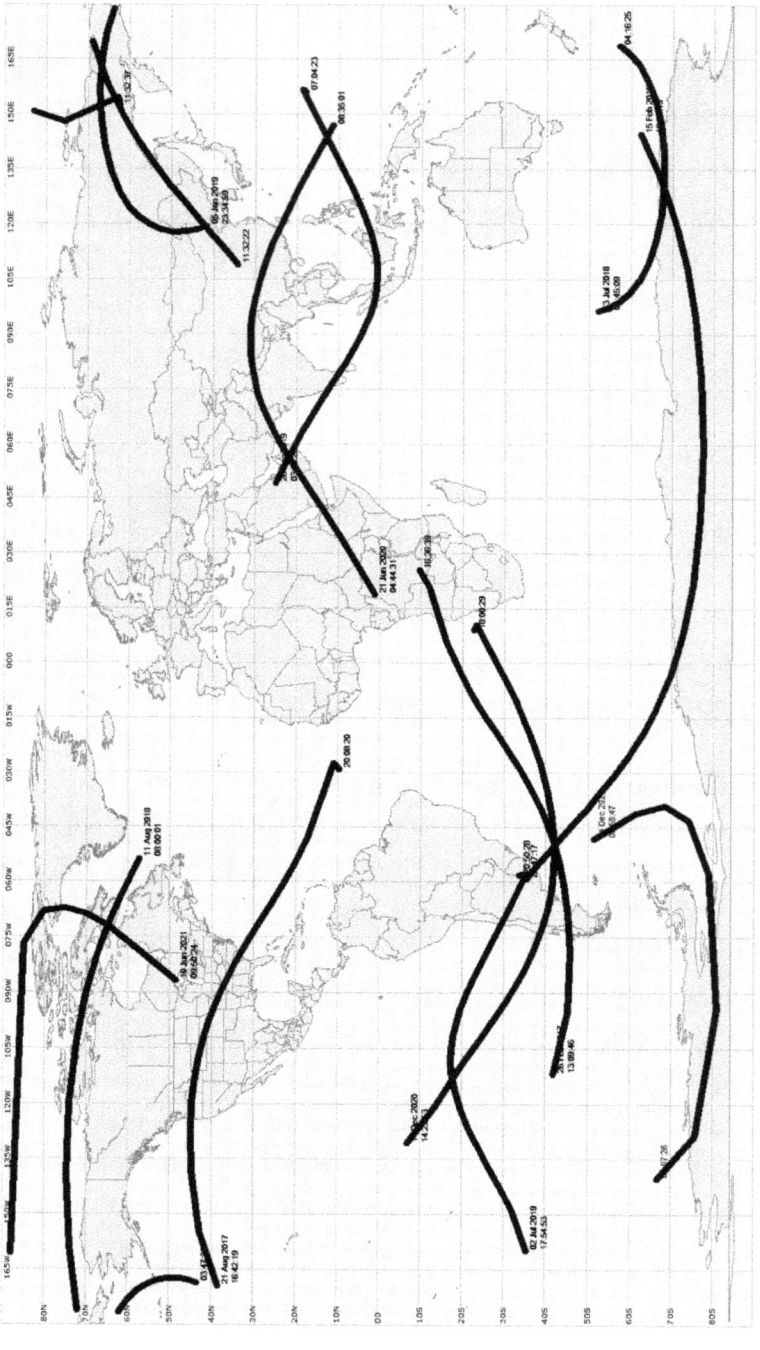

Figure #14 Eclipse Paths

There is a total solar eclipse moving across the United States on August 21, 2017 with a magnitude of 2 min 40 sec.

Three solar eclipses will move across the southern part of South America from 2017, 2019 and 2020 stimulating the exceptionally active seismic activity on the western coast of Peru and Chile as follows:

Feb 26, 2017 – 0 min 44 sc
July 2, 2019 – 4 min 33 sec
Dec 14, 2020 – 2 min 10 sec

On December 26, 2019 an Annular Eclipse with a magnitude of 3 min 39 sec will hit the corner of Saudi Arabia, swoop across the southern tip of India and into the heavy seismic area of the Philippines.

On June 21, 2020 an Annular Eclipse with a magnitude of 00 min 38 sec will begin in Central America through Northern India, Southern China and into the Philippines.

Others close to either the North or South Pole are entering the early part of their long cycle.

The Great San Francisco Earthquake of 1906 (Figure #15)

The eclipse axis of Virgo/Pisces that influenced the Great San Francisco earthquake of April 18, 1906 did not fall across the pertinent Virgo/Pisces eclipse region on the Geodetic map, but in calculating whole charts for the eclipses, we note several important factors:

The eclipse axis lies across the first and seventh houses, but is close to the second and eighth houses of death and economics.

The angles in some areas encompass more than 30 degrees due to the geometric process used to create the cusps. In this case it is the Placidus system. We know some houses are much longer than 30 degrees unless we use whole sign houses.

The South Node of the eclipse directly before this disaster was in Aquarius pulling that region into influence.

During the years of 1903 and 1904 eclipses were moving through Virgo/Pisces, building momentum and triggering many earthquakes in angular positions on the Geodetic Map.

The Great San Francisco Earthquake destroyed much of the city; over 3,000 people died and most of the inhabitants were left homeless. In today's money, the quake caused over eight billion dollars in damage. The shaking was felt as far north as Oregon, south to Los Angeles, and as far inland as Las Vegas. It has been reported that the earth split for 270 miles, and fires raged for several days from broken gas lines. As the city sits on eight faults, another earthquake of similar size could strike at any time with even greater loss of life and property. Every time powerful eclipses fall in their geodetic angles, it is worth noting, particularly those lasting several minutes. However, sometimes a fault has reached a point of extreme weakness and all it takes is a light nudge from a partial eclipse. It seems that planetary influences create a pressure on the earth's skin, but what makes these predictions so difficult is that we cannot gauge the extent of its weakness. All we can do is to note areas and times of potentiality.

Geodetic Astrology for Relocating and World Affairs

THE GREAT SAN FRANCISCO EARTHQUAKE 8.3
April 18, 1906 at 5:12 AM
GEODETIC CUSPS for San Francisco

Inner Wheel: TOTAL SOLAR (E) Aug 30, 1905, Duration 03'46" GMT 13:07:19, SS #143
Outer Wheel: PARTIAL SOLAR (E) Feb 23, 1906, Mag.0.539   GMT 07:43:14, SS #148

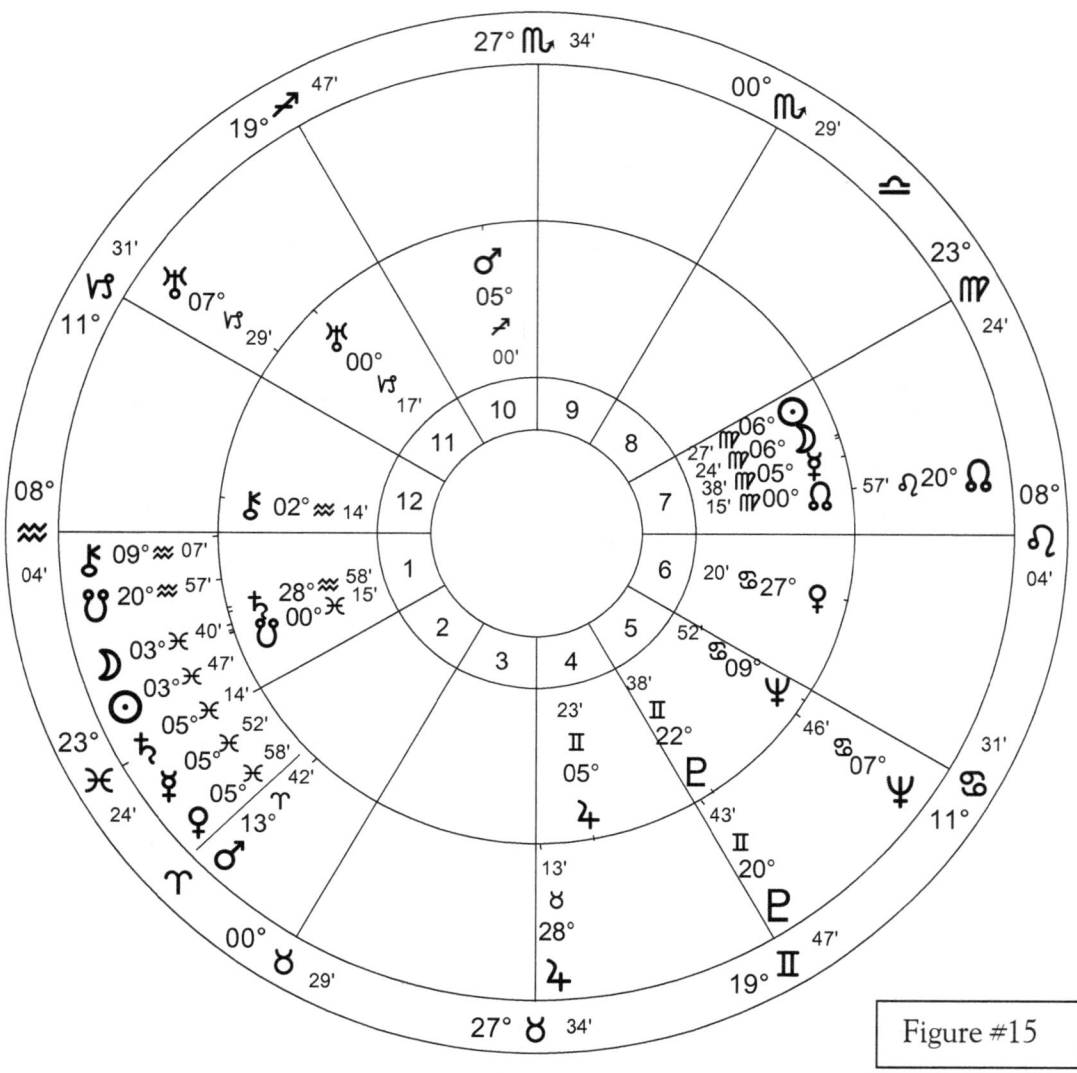

Figure #15

ECLIPSE AXIS: Two solar eclipses about six months apart from 6:27 Virgo to 3:46 Pisces. Eclipses are in angles 1/7 close to 2/8 of death and economics of which both figures were high.

MUTABLE GRAND SQUARE: Inner Mars opposite Jupiter square each eclipse. This sets up the region for some kind of a disaster. One would assume it would be an earthquake due to its active fault line area. Several transits are noted:

T ☉ 27:34 ♈ □ ♀ of inner chart, co-ruler 8th, ☉ ⚻ GE MH Exact
T ☽ 00:01 ♓ ☌ ☊ and ♄ 1st house of inner chart, ⚹ ♅ inner chart ♒ ruler Asc
T ☿ S.D. 07:33 ♈, ruler GE 8th □ ♅ #2 which is ☍ ♆ #2
Previous Full ☽ 18:39 ♎ across houses 2/8. Previous New Moon 02:35 ♉

48

Such energy often triggers weakness in the tectonic plates in other areas, as well as those in close proximity, such as the Great Quake that struck Valparaiso, Chili on August 17, 1906 with a magnitude of 8.2 when 20,000 people perished. Valparaiso has a Midheaven of 18:26 Capricorn and an Ascendant of 16:59 Aries, which means the Virgo/Pisces eclipses did not fall in their geodetic angles. The Virgo/Pisces eclipses began across Valparaiso's sixth/twelfth houses, moved backwards into its fifth/eleventh, and then on July 21, just 26 days prior to the quake, an eclipse landed in its fourth house at 28 Cancer. It was an unusual eclipse pattern with two solar eclipses about thirty days apart rather than the usual six months. This was preceded by a Full Moon in the tenth house. Transiting Saturn, ruler of the Midheaven, made a trine to the eighth cusp. Then, transiting Mars, the ascendant ruler, coupled with Mercury to square the eighth house.

In the same area, on January 31, 1906 off the coast of Ecuador, an earthquake erupted with a magnitude of 8.6. The death toll was estimated at 1,000.

On August 5, 1906 the Italian steamer *Sirio* was wrecked off the coast of Spain, and 350 people went down with it. The Midheaven of that area is Pisces.

On April 4, 1905 Jammu and Kashmir, India, experienced a 7.8 magnitude. The death toll was 19,000.

The Great Chilean Earthquake of 1960 Magnitude 9.5 (Figure #16)

The largest earthquake ever recorded occurred off the coast of Chile. It lasted ten minutes, creating enormous tsunamis that swept the coastline of South America, north to California, Oregon, Alaska, the Hawaiian Islands and even Japan, with waves about six meters high. It was also felt in Australia and New Zealand. It was called The Great Pacific Tsunami.

Off the coast of South America, the tsunami waves were as high as 25 meters (82 feet) sinking boats, destroying property, and leaving an estimated 2,000,000 homeless. The death toll was difficult to estimate but altogether between the quake and the tsunamis, anywhere from 3,000 to 6,000 people perished.

It took about fifteen hours for the tsunami to hit the Hawaiian Islands where most of the damage occurred in Hilo Bay on the island of Hawaii. Here the waves reached about 35 feet destroying the waterfront and reaching far inland. When I was there in 1979 people were still talking about it, pointing out landmarks, and explaining how the newly built sea wall in the harbour would break some of the power of a future tsunami.

As far away as Japan, waves reached higher than six feet creating the greatest damage and loss of life along the coast of Honshu. The death toll was estimated at 199, with many missing and injured and over 1500 homes destroyed. The total damage was around $50 million in 1960 dollars.

The earthquake itself altered the shoreline of Chile, creating landslides, rock falls, and a new lake. Within 47 hours after the main earthquake, the Puyahue volcano erupted creating a plume of gas and ash about eight kilometers high. There was no reported damage or loss of life due to its interior mountain location.

After-shocks continued for a month. At least a couple of these aftershocks measured 7.0 or over on the Richter scale.

Geodetic Astrology for Relocating and World Affairs

THE GREAT CHILEAN EARTHQUAKE 9.5
May 22, 1960 at 3:11 PM Local Time
GEODETIC CUSPS for center of earthquake Valdivia, Chile

Inner Wheel: TOTAL SOLAR (E) Oct 2, 1959, Duration 3'02" GMT 12:26:27 SS #143
Outer Wheel: PARTIAL SOLAR (E) Mar 27, 1960, Mag 0.706 GMT 07:24:34 SS #148

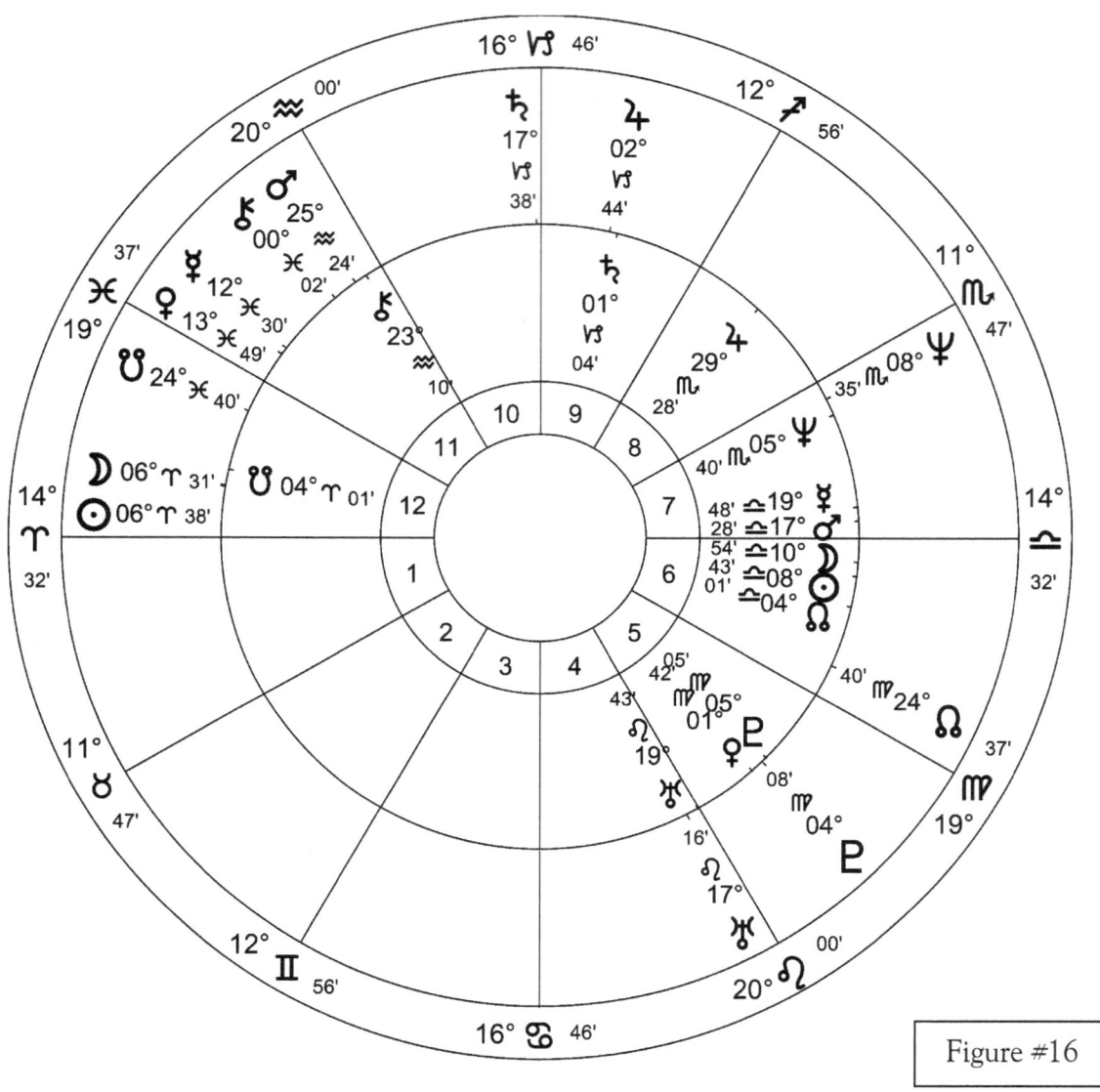

Figure #16

ECLIPSE AXIS: across Libra/Aries, much less than 10 degrees in separation, setting up a location for a major event. The earthquake hit at the most vulnerable area along the edge of two plates. Note Mars and Mercury conjoining the inner eclipse, and Saturn conj GE MC forming a T-Square. Notable transits are as follows:

T ☉ 1:40 ♊ ☍ inner Saturn, ruler MC, and Jupiter
T ♄ 17:55 ♑ ℞ remains ☌ MC
T ☽ 1:07 ♉ △ inner ♄, apex T □
T ♂ 8:43 ♈ ☌ eclipse ruling GE Asc
T ♆ 7:07 ♏ ℞ ☍ 2nd eclipse

If the geodetic angles have any meaning in determining seismic activity, we can expect other occurrences wherever the Virgo/Pisces signs are in angles on the Geodetic map. Such is the case on February 29, 1960 when an earthquake of 5.7 on the Richer ccale hit Agadir, Morocco. It has an MC/IC axis in Pisces/Virgo respectively. The quake was not large by measurement but tens of thousands were reported dead, thousands were injured, and many more were left homeless.

In November 1960, a 7.6 Earthquake occurred off the coast of Peru, creating tsunamis 30 feet high.

Several severe cyclones hit the North Indian Ocean during the 1960 cyclone season with an estimated 20,000 dead. The Geodetic axis here is Virgo/Pisces on the Ascendant/Descendent axis.

Good Friday Alaskan Earthquake of 1964 Magnitude 9.2 (Figure #17)

This is another of the three or four greatest earthquakes ever recorded in the world to date with a measurement of 9.2 on the Richter scale with about 42 aftershocks. It was initially measured at 8.7 then upgraded according to studied seismic activity. Wikipedia Encyclopedia quotes, "evidence of motion directly related to the quake was reported from all over the world."

Eye witness accounts report that the land rolled and rippled like an ocean. Buildings toppled like toys, fissures opened up engulfing people. In downtown Anchorage fissures opened as wide as fifty feet and as deep as twelve feet, dropping buildings, cars, and anything else that was upon it. For 4 minutes and 38 seconds, over a distance of 500 miles across the State, the land twisted, rolled and heaved. Harbors drained of water, only to have it flung back with incredible force. Some areas were raised as much as 90 feet (9.1 meters) while other areas dropped by 8 feet (2.4 meters). Tidal waves in Alaska reached incredible heights of 67 meters (220 feet), then rushed down the coast of North America to California and over the Pacific Ocean to Hawaii and Japan.

Tsunamis as high as 12 to 15 feet hit the California coast causing extensive flooding, considerable damage, and killing over 100 people. The speed of the water as it hit the California coast was measured at 500 miles per hour. Even as far as Houston, Texas a peculiar shockwave was reported causing a freakish high tide two days later, according to the New York Times.

Some ground areas were permanently raised by 30 feet (9.1 meters). Other areas dropped permanently by 8 feet.

Property damage in Alaska was estimated at over $300 million, but as incredible as it may seem, only about 139 people perished. Had this quake occurred in a densely populated area, the loss of life would have been staggering.

On the 2-wheel eclipse charts, Figure #17, note the axis position of the eclipses. Both are angular, which is so often the case for the largest earthquakes, but this is another that shows one eclipse close to the second and eighth house divisions that involve economics and loss of life. Eclipse axis degrees can show an area of vulnerability but the exact location is dependent upon the spot of seismic weakness.

Probably the greatest single factor contributing to the energy build-up is the forming of the Great Conjunction of Uranus and Pluto in 1965, particularly in areas where it squares an ascendant of Gemini/Sagittarius, as it does in the following chart of the Great Alaskan Earthquake of 1964. It

Geodetic Astrology for Relocating and World Affairs

THE GOOD FRIDAY GREAT ALASKAN EARTHQUAKE 9.2
March 28, 1964 at 5:36 PM PST
GEODETIC CUSPS for epicentre of the Earthquake

Inner Wheel: TOTAL SOLAR (E) Jul 20, 1963, Duration 1'40" GMT 20:35:37 SS #145
Outer Wheel: PARTIAL SOLAR (E) Jan 14, 1964, Mag. 0.559 GMT 20:29:31 SS #150

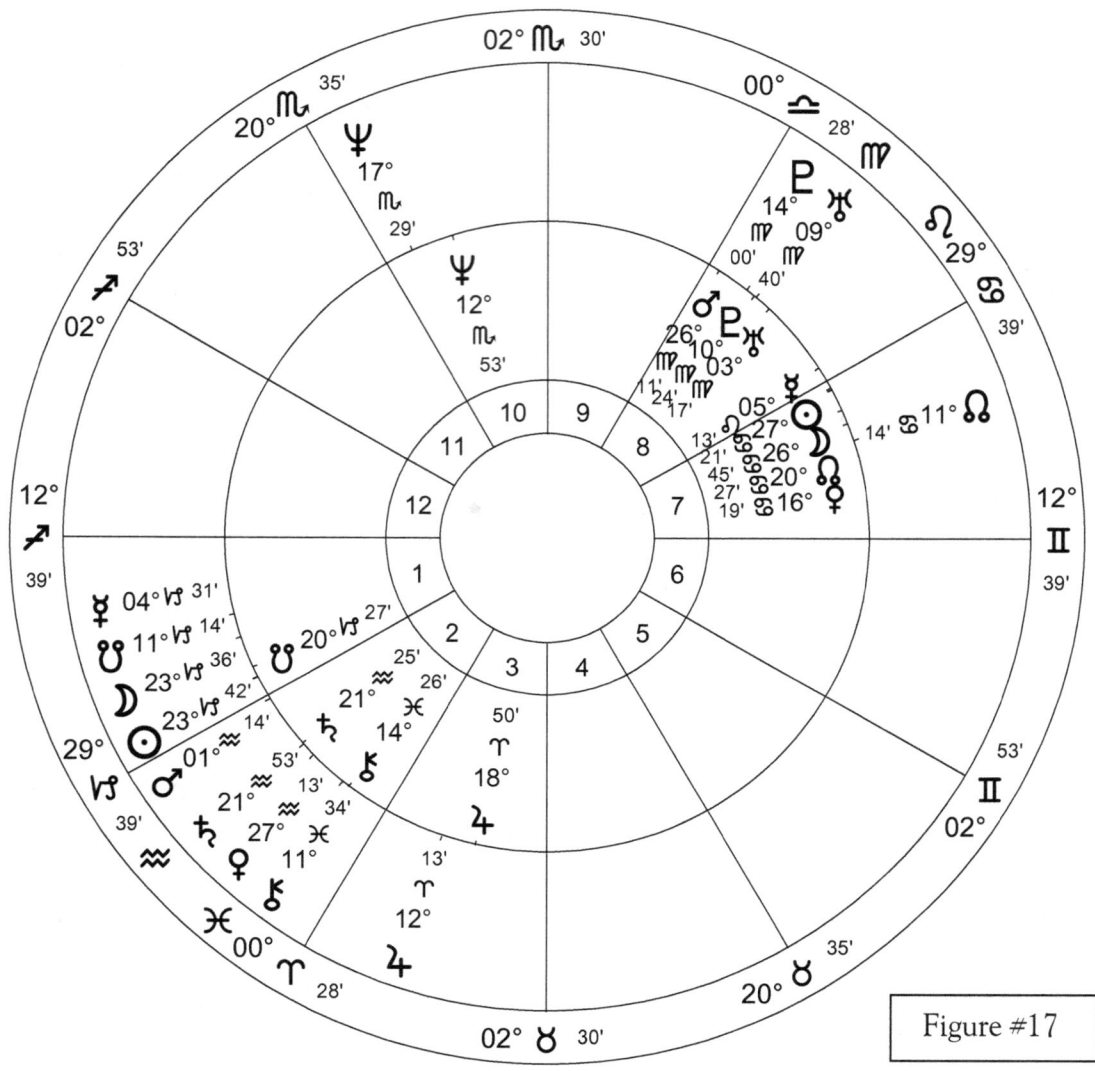

Figure #17

An earthquake occurs in the spot of greatest weakness on the fault. This is where two great plates grind against each other. Note Mars close to the eclipse on outer chart prior to the quake.

Previous New ☽ March 14, 1964 at 23:32 ♓ ✶ outer eclipse at 23:42 ♑. Other notable transits as follows:

T ♂ 28:55 ♓ △ inner eclipse 27:21 ♋
T ☿ 21:43 ♈ □ ☊ inner chart, ✶ ♄
T ☉ 07:24 ♈
T ♃ 26:24 ♈, Ruler Asc. □ both eclipses, ⚻ inner chart ♂
T ♇ 12:19 ♍ ℞ □ Asc/Desc, ✶ ♆ inner chart, ✶ ☊ outer chart, ⚻ outer chart ♃

52

indicates that during the mid 1960s there would have been an unusual number of disasters, particularly along applicable geodetic angles. It is also understandable that earthquakes would occur about 180 degrees away on the other side of our planet. The map does not show the number of degrees in the angles due to interceptions in calculations, so it is advisable to ascertain the exact geodetic cusps to see where the strongest eclipse energy bears down. Such is the area of Japan, where the Uranus/Pluto conjunction occurred in the tenth house indicating another area of extreme vulnerability and activity. The Niigata Japan Earthquake is a perfect example. It is shown in Figure #18. As mentioned above, 1964 was a memorable year for disastrous events, notably earthquakes, and storms that will be dealt with in the next chapter. Along with the building of the Uranus/Pluto conjunction at 16/17 degrees Virgo, it was an unusual year with four partial solar eclipses, as follows:

January 14, 1964 Partial Solar (E) Magnitude 0.559, 23:43 Capricorn, SS #150 (Relatively new)

June 10, 1964 Partial Solar (E) Magnitude 0.0755, 19:19 Gemini, SS #117 (Old, Winding down)

July 9, 1964 Partial Solar (E) Magnitude 0.322, 17:15 Cancer, SS #155 (Just forming)

December 4, 1964 Partial Solar (E) Magnitude 0.752, 11:56 Sagittarius, SS #122 (Quite old)

The implication here is that the solar eclipses are moving backwards in their usual fashion, from Cancer/Capricorn to Gemini/Sagittarius, sensitizing those geodetic angles, along with the mutable degrees of the Great Conjunction. The Gemini/Sagittarius eclipses continue as total eclipses into 1965 with much longer periods of duration of over four and five minutes each. This indicates that 1965 would unfold with many memorable events including earthquakes and storms.

A few other interesting unusual incidents warrant mention:

It is hard to imagine how two naval ships can collide on a clear day but they did in February 1964 in the Gulf of Aden in the Indian Ocean. All four of the geodetic angles for that location are mutable.

In Montana, USA, the worst flooding in history was experienced under the Sagittarius/Gemini MC/IC.

Africa is basically under a Cancer/Capricorn Ascendant/Descendant. Nelson Mandela was sentenced to life imprisonment in 1964 under this influence. He had a Cancer Sun.

In Lima, Peru, in May 1964, under the Capricorn Midheaven, the worst stadium disaster in the world occurred, in which 300 people were killed.

Earthquakes in Japan

Japan is wedged precisely between two very large tectonic plates that grind against each other, making the country particularly prone to very large earthquakes. It is also part of the highly volatile Pacific Fire Circle, as previously mentioned.

As an example, on September 1, 1923 an enormous upheaval well over 8+ on the Richter scale hit the heavily populated cities of Tokyo and Yokohama, leaving them in ruins. Over 140,000 people

Geodetic Astrology for Relocating and World Affairs

NIIGATA JAPAN EQARTHQUAKE MAGNITUDE 7.5
June 16, 1964 at 01:01 PM Local Time
GEODETIC CUSPS EPICENTRE 38N22 139E22

Inner Wheel: PARTIAL SOLAR (E) Jan 14, 1964, Mag. 0.559 GMT 20:29:31 SS #150
Outer Wheel: PARTIAL SOLAR (E) Jun 10, 1964, Mag. 0.755 GMT 4:33:33 SS #117

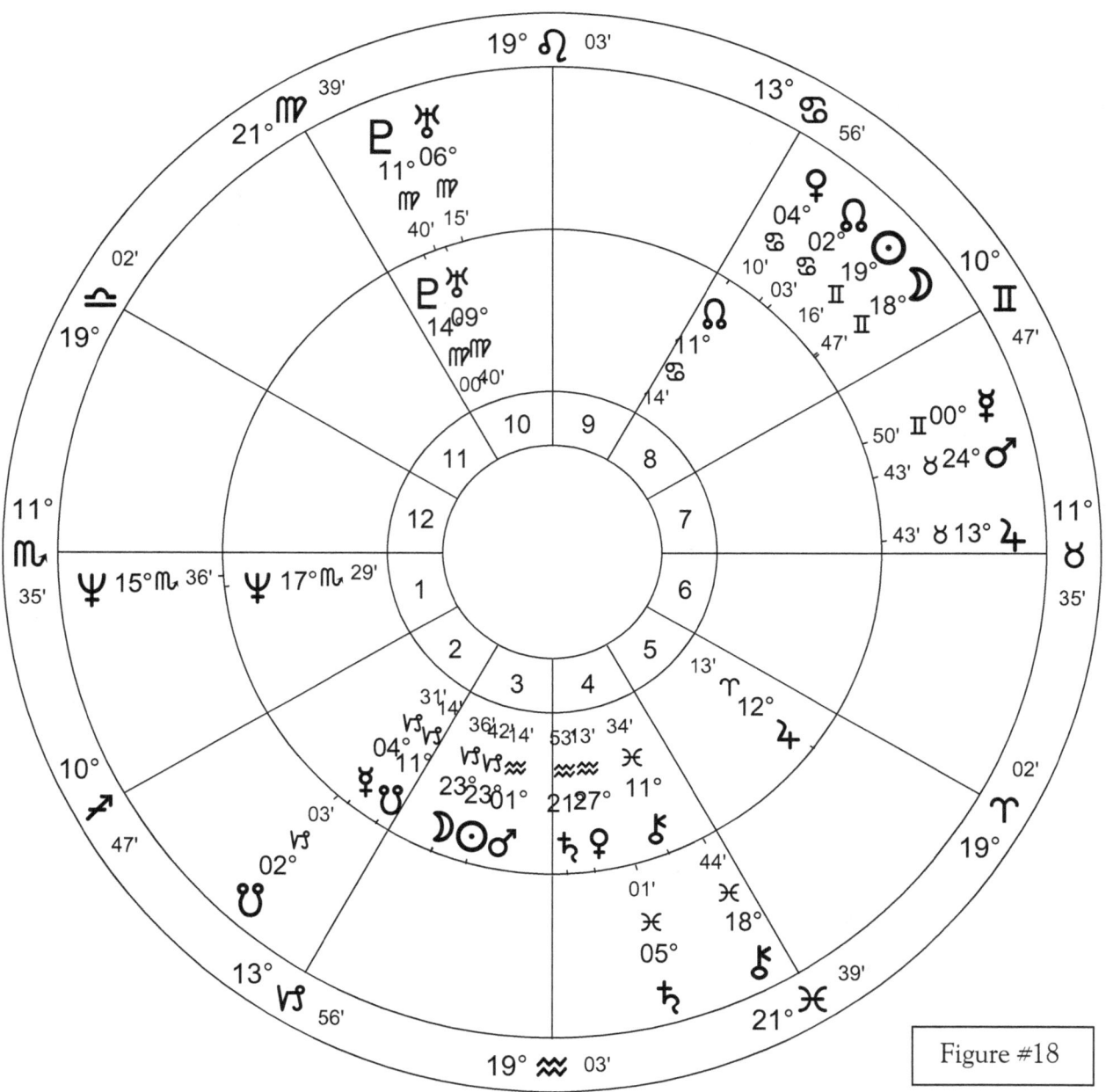

Figure #18

♇ ☌ ♅ in 10th
Inner eclipse chart ♄ ☌ GE 4th
Previous New ☽ June 10, 1964 19:19 ♊ in GE 8th
T ☿ 12:40 ♊ ruler 8th ☌ GE 8th

fell into fissures, were tossed about, crushed, burned or electrocuted. In 2011 an earthquake over 9 in intensity hit at a point on the Pacific side of the main island of Honshu near the Fukushima Daiichi nuclear power plant. See Figure #22.

Niigata, Japan, Earthquake of June 16, 1964 Magnitude 7.5 (Figure #18)

It is fortunate that earthquakes of huge magnitude do not occur very often and sometimes they happen in less densely populated areas such as the 7.5 quake in 1964 that took place under the powerful mutable planetary picture. It is often referred to as the Niigata Earthquake because that is the name of the city where most of the damage occurred. The epicentre was fifty miles from Niigata in the Sea of Japan at a depth of about 57 km below sea level.

Fortunately only about 36 died and 385 were injured; there was damage to houses and other buildings, including the destruction of seven bridges. This was due mainly due to the subsoil rather than the vibration of the quake as much of the town was built on a thick layer of sand compaction.

As the Great Conjunction of Uranus/Pluto became exact in 1965/1966, and solar eclipses shifted first across Gemini/Sagittarius, then across Taurus/Scorpio, many disasters accumulated on record along those eclipse paths. Here are a few of them:

Rat Island Earthquake, in the Aleutian Island Chain
February 4, 1965, Magnitude 8.7 with a strong tsunami.

Oaxaca, Mexico Earthquake
August 23, 1965, 7.5. It was considered a small thrust in which the little Cocos Plate slid under the North American Plate. Five people were killed due to the location.

Coram Sea, Indonesia
January 24, 1965, Magnitude 8.2: 71 dead, 3,000 buildings and 14 bridges destroyed.

Biah, Indonesia
February 17, 1996, Magnitude 8.1: 108 dead.

Puget Sound area, Washington State
April 29, 1965, 8:29 AM PDT Magnitude 6.5
It killed seven people and caused about $12.5 million dollars in property damage. It was also felt in the neighboring States of Oregon, Idaho, Montana and in the Province of British Columbia.

Tornado Alley
In early May 1965 there was an unusual number of excessively violent tornado outbreaks right up through central United States to the Upper Midwest across the Great Plains states, and as far as the Dakotas. This is an area often referred to as Tornado Alley. The storms lasted for three days and produced tornadoes from F2+ to F4–F5, according to news reports at the time. The Geodetic angles in this region are Gemini/Sagittarius as well as Virgo/Pisces, putting the Great Conjunction of Uranus/Pluto right on the seventh house cusp throughout much of that region. The eclipse axis during this period was across Gemini/Sagittarius, geodetically right up the Geodetic Sagittarius Midheaven.

On the other side of the world, with reverse cusps, similar storms were sweeping the planet...

The Anatolian Fault in Turkey (Figure #19)

The Anatolian Fault in Turkey is one of the biggest in the world, comparable to the San Andreas Fault in California with similar features. It basically runs east and west as well as north and south through the country. It is tucked between the large Eurasian Plate and the small Arabian Plate. It is highly active having produced no less than seven Major Earthquakes from 1939 to 1967 well over 7+ on the Richter scale.

On August 17, 1999 at 3:01 AM Local Time an earthquake of 7.4 occurred at an epicentre very close to Ismit, as marked on the above diagram. A memorable total solar eclipse occurred just six days prior on August 11 with a grand fixed square and duration of 2 minutes 23 seconds. The path of that eclipse started just off the Eastern Coast of Canada, swept across the Atlantic, over the United Kingdom, through Europe, and right through Ismit and along that very fault line. No wonder the death toll was estimated at well over 30,000 with a similar number injured.

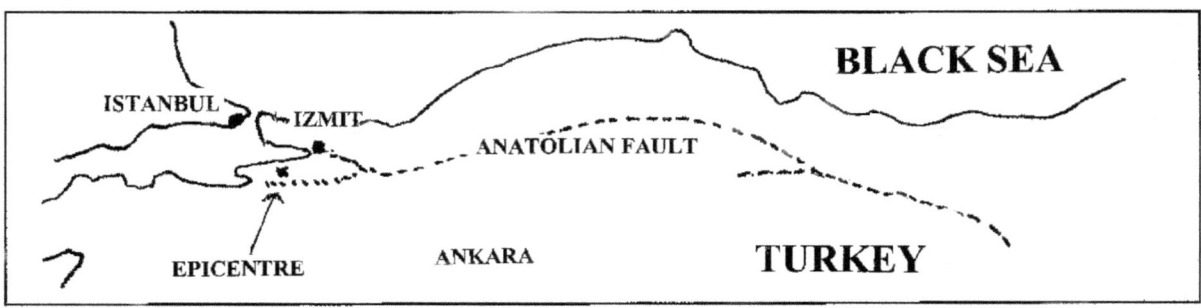

Figure #19 Anatolian Fault

Mexico City Earthquake of 1985 Magnitude 8.1 (Figure #20)

This is called the Mexico City earthquake even though its epicentre was located about 350 kilometres (220 miles) out in the Pacific Ocean. The severity of the earthquake and the damage caused is the reason for its name. It was also accompanied by two aftershocks of magnitude 7+ causing continued damage to an already ravaged area.

The city was originally built on an island in the middle of Lake Texcoco and the lake was eventually drained, but the lake bed was made of soft clay from volcanic ash with a high water content, which added to the seismic shaking and movement. Reports indicate that the ground shook for more than five minutes in some places.

The main center of the eruption occurred in a very active location where the North America Plate bumps into the little Cocos and Pacific Plate. In Figure #13 you can see the small plate tucked in just above the active Nazca Plate. The power generated reached as far as Los Angeles and Houston, Texas.

The estimate of those perished was at least 10,000 but perhaps as high as 45,000 due to bodies never recovered in the rubble. According to government figures, around 250,000 lost their homes. The cost was estimated between three and four billion US dollars.

Geophysical Disruptions

MEXICO CITY EARTHQUAKE OF 1985 MAGNITUDE 8.1
September 19, 1985 at 7:19 AM CST
GEODETIC CUSPS EPICENTRE IN PACIFIC OCEAN 17N36, 102W30

Inner Wheel: TOTAL SOLAR (E) Nov 22, 1984, Duration 1'60" GMT 22.53.22 SS #142
Outer Wheel: PARTIAL SOLAR (E) May 19, 1985, Mag. 0.841 GMT 21:28:42 SS #147

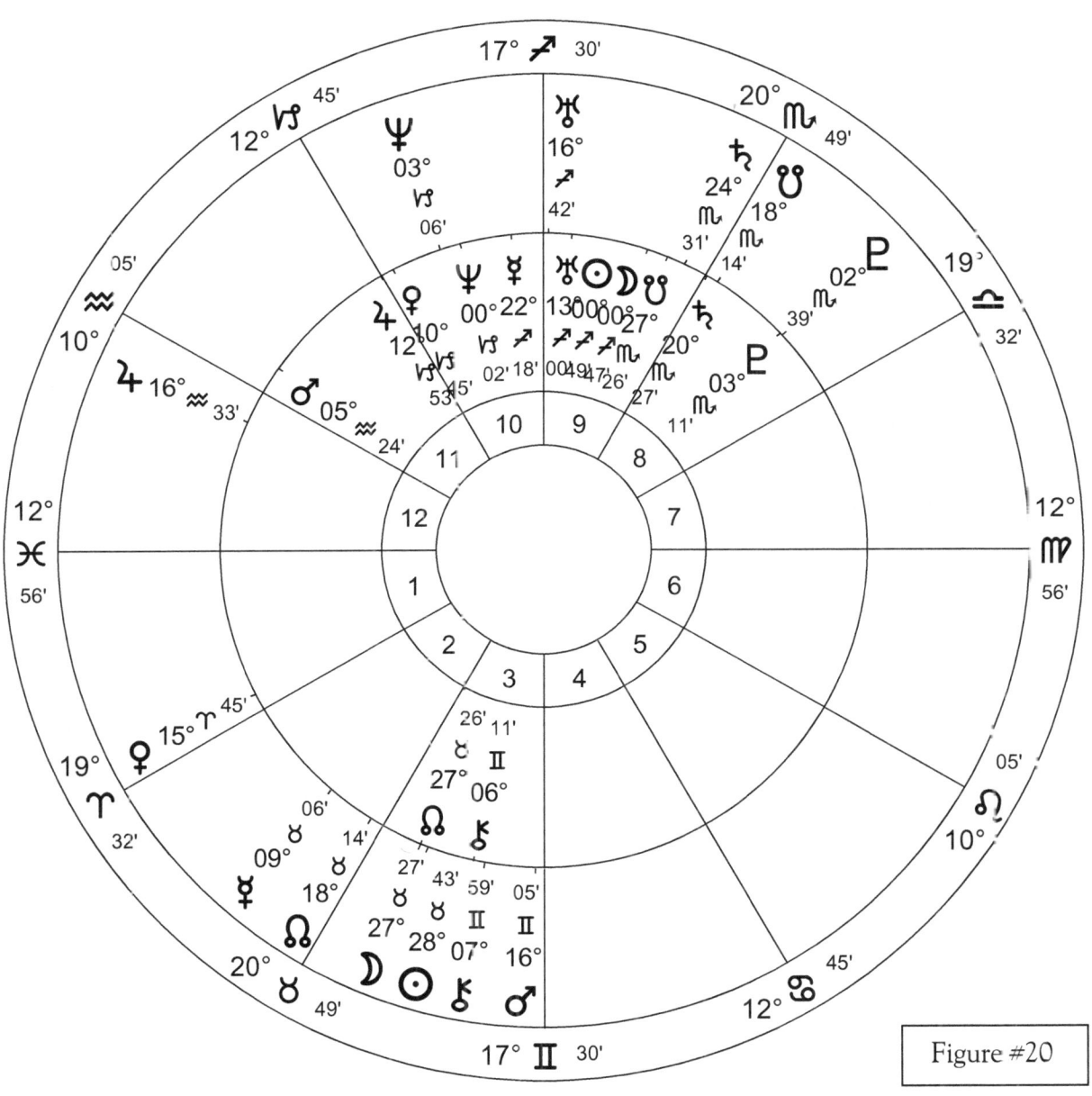

Figure #20

Note outer eclipse chart: ♂ ☌ IC and ♅ ☌ MC
Prev. New ☽ 21:55 ♍ □ inner ☿ and MC/IC
Transits: T ♂ 6:00 ♍ ⚻ inner ♂
T ♄ 23:51 ♏ ☌ outer ♄
T ♀ 26:52 ♌ □ inner ☊ and outer ☽
T ☊ 09:51 ♉ ☌ outer ☿

The Sumatra/Indian Ocean Mega Earthquake/Tsunami of 2004 9.1–9.3 (Figure #21)

The epicentre of this earthquake occurred off the west coast of Sumatra, Indonesia, with a resulting tsunami that reached many countries bordering on the Indian Ocean. The shaking continued for ten minutes with a seismic oscillation between 8–10 inches. The result was felt throughout India, Thailand, Singapore, and triggering other earthquakes as far away as Alaska. Faults kept actually "popping up" parts of the sea floor which greatly increased both the height and speed of the waves that reached as high as 30 meters (100 feet) in some communities.

As coastal waters quickly inundated coastal land masses, over 230,000 people lost their lives. The devastation was so massive that it is impossible to estimate the destruction and monetary value, or even the number of lives lost. It takes many years for recovery, if ever. Entire families and communities were wiped out.

It is certainly classed as one of the three or four largest earthquakes ever recorded including the Good Friday Earthquake in Alaska in 1964, The Great Chilean Earthquake of 1960, and the 2011 Earthquake in Japan that caused radiation fallout.

This particular earthquake was the result of the complex action between the Indian, Burma and Australian Tectonic Plates. The Indian Plate is actually part of the much larger Eurasian Plate, which seems to be pushing under the Burma Plate. Also, it was discovered that there were two ruptures that were nearly two minutes apart. The first one was very fast and opened up large fissures many miles beneath the sea bed, which is what would have likely caused the popping up of the sea floor. The second one was much slower in an area where the quake changed to a slipping movement as two plates moved in opposite directions.

Tsunamis connected with this earthquake were particularly powerful and devastating, with waves reaching as far away as Mexico, Chile and the Arctic. It triggered outer quakes as far away as Alaska. It is not hard to imagine that it would have weakened other fault lines in various geographic locations bringing their next slippage forward to a closer date. This and powerful planetary energies working together can stimulate very large eruptions. It may have hastened the earthquake that occurred on October 8, 2005 in Pakistan where those same plates were active, along with the October 3 annular solar eclipse with a duration of 4 minutes 31 seconds. More than 80,000 perished and more than 2.5 million were left homeless. It is also under the same Geodetic angles of Aries/Libra where solar eclipses continued in Aries/Libra throughout all of 2005 and to March 29 of 2006.

Also, on March 28, 2005, another earthquake occurred off the west coast of Sumatra, this time measuring 8.6 on the Richter scale, and a little further north. Seismologists did not consider it to be an aftershock of its forerunner on December 26, 2004, but it is reasonable to assume that the affecting faults were weakened or jarred to some extent. It lasted for two minutes, with numerous aftershocks up to 5.5 and 6.0. The death toll was estimated to be at least one thousand.

With these two hits so close together, the city of Band Aceh and surrounding communities had no opportunity to recover from the first when the second one was on them. This second earthquake was not quite as strong as that in 2004, due to a little lesser magnitude and being a little further north.

Geophysical Disruptions

MEGATHRUST SUMATRA/INDIAN OCEAN EARTHQUAKE/TSUNAMI 9.1-9.3
December 26, 2004, 7:58:53 AM Local Time
GEODETIC CUSPS FOR BANDA ACEH, INDONESIA (Close to Epicentre)

Inner Wheel: PARTIAL SOLAR (E), Apr 19, 2004   Mag. 0.737   GMT 13:34:05   SS #119
Outer Wheel: PARTIAL SOLAR (E), Oct. 14, 2004   Mag. 0.928   GMT 02:59:22   SS #124

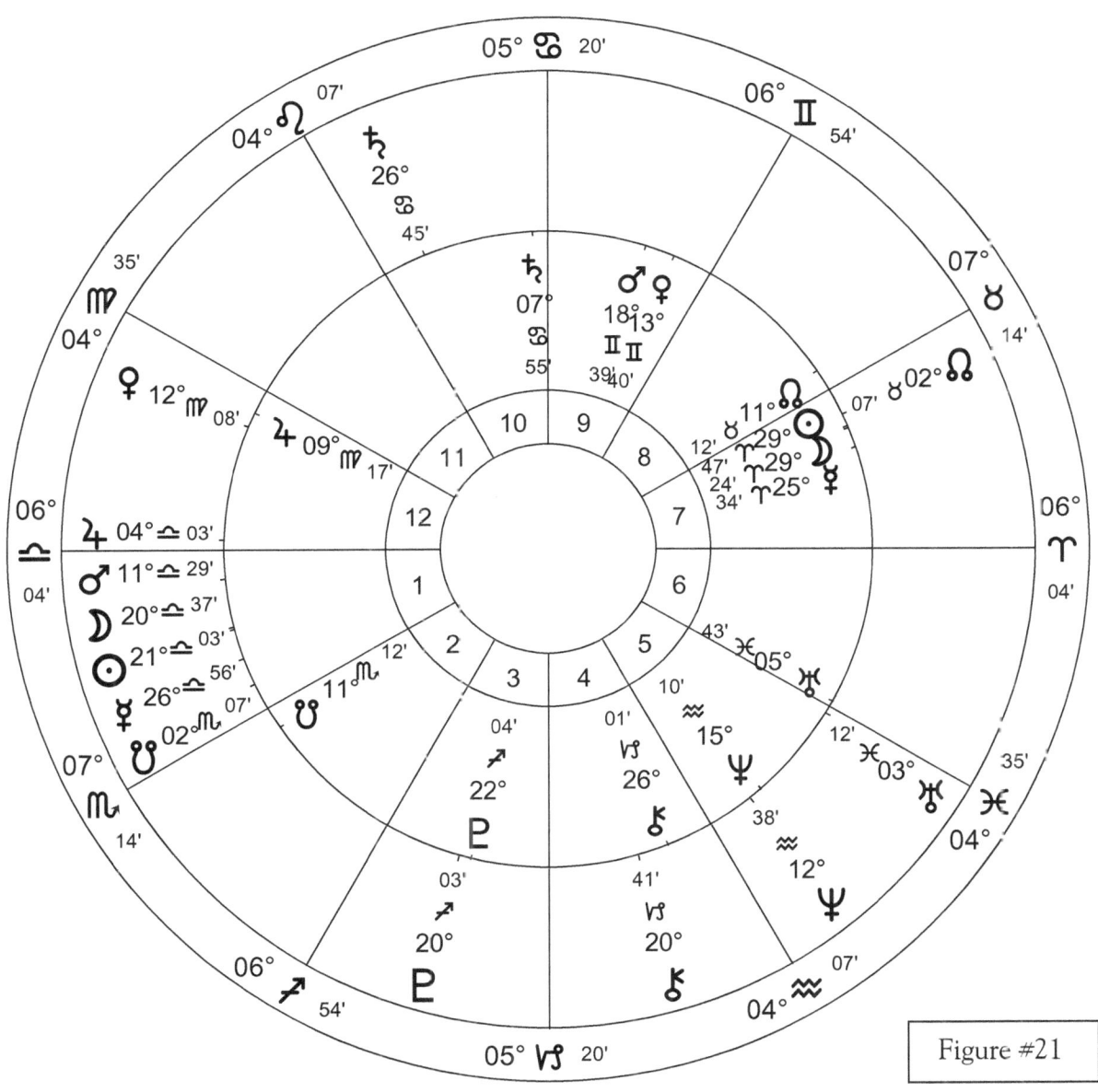

Figure #21

Eclipses are angular and close to 2/8 – ☊ leading in 2/8.
This often happens in disaster charts when losses are high in both lives and cost.
Previous New ☽ Dec 12, 20:22 ♐ ☌ ♇
Outer chart ♃ ☌ Asc. and moving into an angular position
Transits: T ♄ on midpoint of both eclipses
T ♂ 28:53 ♏ ☍ inner eclipse

The Great Tohoku Earthquake of 2011 Magnitude 9.0 (Figure #22) and Fukushima Reactor Accidents of 2011

This is the fourth largest earthquake in recorded history and occurred on March 11, 2011, at 2:46:23 PM JST, in the Pacific Ocean off the coast of Honshu, in the district of Tohoku. The epicentre was approximately 70 kilometers (43 miles) off the coast, at a depth of approximately 30 kilometers (19 miles). The tsunamis created reached heights of 40.5 meters (133 feet), sweeping the shore and travelling many miles inland.

As I study the Geodetic map location of the pair of eclipses in houses directly prior to this devastating event, I must admit that I would not have been alerted to this geodetic location just by looking at the map. In presenting speculative concepts, one can only choose those charts that exhibit the strongest examples but sooner or later we must look at these situations for what they may or may not present to us. In looking at the Geodetic map it would not be difficult to see that the eclipses across Cancer/Capricorn would only be one sign away from the Leo/Aquarius Midheaven and could therefore lie across the second/eighth houses in the full Geodetic chart, representing very large loss of life. Also, the eighth house has a certain relationship to atomic energy and the transformation that can arise out of rubble and destruction. Figure #22 shows eclipses across the third and ninth houses, bordering on the eighth. It is an opportunity for additional study and can add to a workable knowledge base.

The coordinates for this chart were purposely chosen for Fukushima, the nuclear reactor site, rather than for the earthquake epicentre. It only makes a difference of one or two degrees on both the angles and intermediary cusps in the Placidus system.

The death toll mounted to over 15,000 with thousands more injured or missing. Over 125,000 buildings were destroyed, and over a million buildings severely damaged, suspending factory production and other services. Many have been forced into bankruptcy. Food and water were severely limited resulting in survivors who died in shelters or while being evacuated. Losses from the earthquake alone have been estimated at billions of dollars to say nothing of the nuclear disaster where the clean up will likely take decades.

The resulting earthquake created a tsunami that caused unprecedented damage to the Fukushima Daiichi Nuclear Power Plant that released severe radioactivity into the air, ground and ocean waters. The reactors that were built on this earthquake-sensitive hot spot were thought to be sufficiently reinforced and not as vulnerable to extreme seismic activity as other areas in Japan. Large earthquakes seemed more likely to occur in the southerly regions of Japan, such as the devastating Tokyo and Yokahama 8.3 quake of 1923, and the major quakes on the island of Hokkaido where tremors from 5–6 happened very frequently. In 1993 Hokkaido experienced a 7.7 earthquake and in 2003 another at 8.3.

The geography of the earth has also been altered by this thrust. Japan is 2.4 meters (7.9 feet) closer to North America than it was before the event, and some areas of Japan are now wider. The Pacific Plate may have moved at least 20 meters (66 feet) westward, if not further. It is also estimated that the earth's axis has shifted anywhere from 10–25 centimetres (4–10 inches). That also affects the Chandler wobble and the earth's rotational rate. One wonders what will unfold from this.

Geophysical Disruptions

THE GREAT TOHOKU EARTHQUAKE OF 2011 MAGNITUDE 9.0 AND FUKUSHIMA REACTOR ACCIDENTS
March 11, 2011 at 2:46:23 PM
Geodetic Cusps Fukushima, Japan

Inner Wheel: TOTAL SOLAR (E) July 11, 2010, Duration 5'20" GMT 19:33:37 SS #146
Outer Wheel: PARTIAL SOLAR (E) Jan. 4, 2011, Mag 0.858   GMT 08:50:42 SS #151

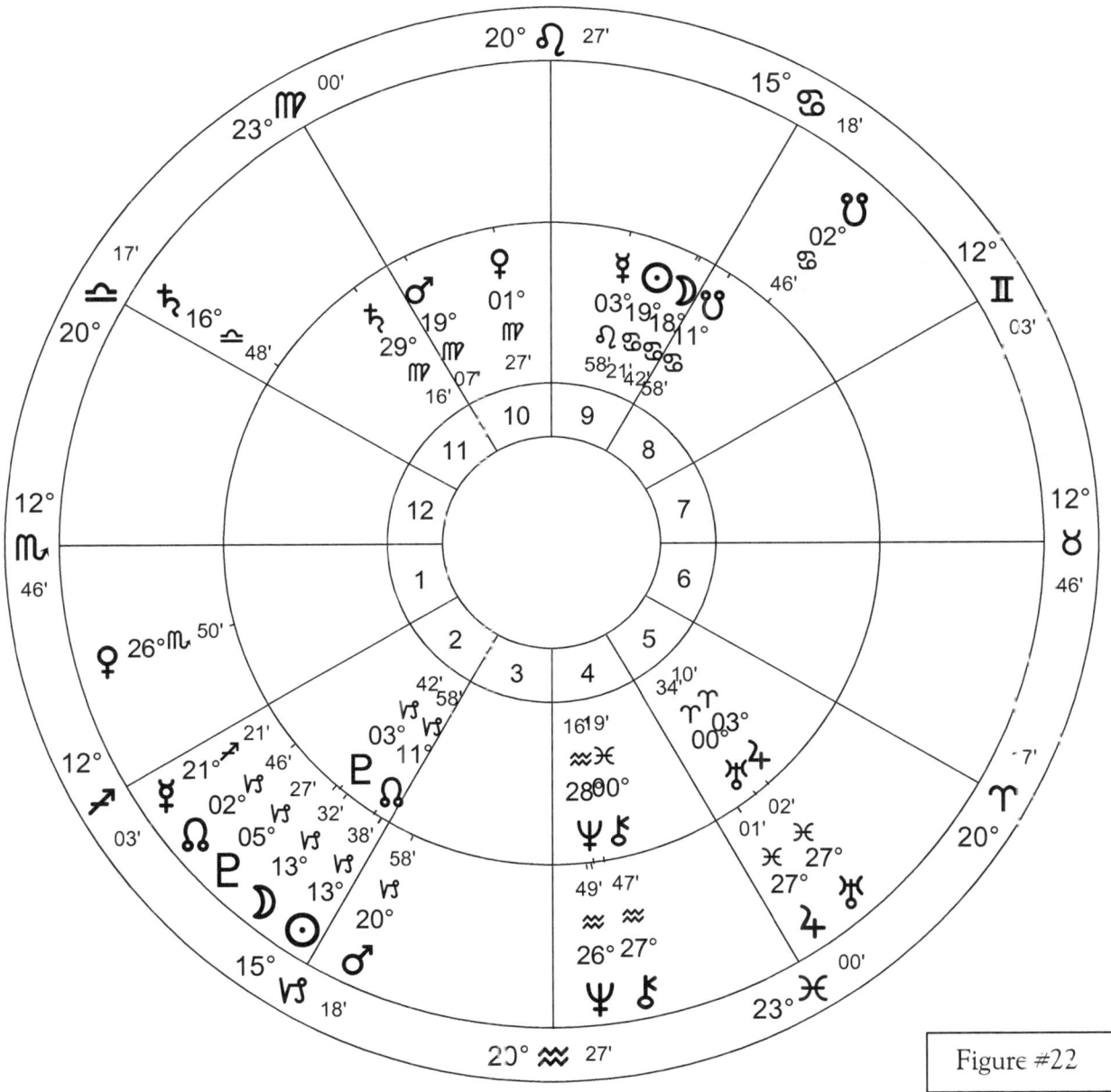

Figure #22

Both eclipses conj 2/8 axis of death, destruction and economics

Previous Full ☽ Feb 18, 2011 29:20 ♌ in GE 10th house ☍ inner chart ♆
Previous New ☽ March 4, 2011 13:56 ♓ △ GE Asc
Transits: T ☉ 20:18 ♓ ⚼ GE MC
T ♂ 12:46 ♓ exactly △ GE Asc

Volcanic Activity

A volcanic eruption is an awesome and terrifying spectacle exhibiting and exposing the immense fiery nature that lies deep within the earth. There are vents or fissures on the surface of the earth where enormous quantities of steam, molten rock, ash, and various gases are blown into the heavens, often accompanied by hot lava running down the sides of the mountain, covering and burning the countryside.

There are approximately 1500–1900 active volcanoes in the world today, three-quarters of which lie within the Pacific Fire Circle. About 50–70 erupt every year and about 20 are erupting at any given time. About 500 million people live close to active volcanoes. Prominent volcanic areas along the Pacific Fire Circle's rim are located in Indonesia, Japan, Central America, the Aleutian Islands of Alaska, the Hawaiian islands and Iceland. The most active volcanoes are located along major fault lines where two tectonic plates rubbing together can create enough heat to melt the rock on the earth's crust where it sometimes becomes thinner from the rubbing process. The molten lava or magma that is released then solidifies and forms a mountain or characteristic cone with a hollow summit or crater.

There are different kinds of volcanoes based upon their characteristics. The Stratovolcano is the classic cone shape with steep sloping sides like Mount Vesuvius, which erupted in 79 AD killing 20,000–25,000 people and burying two cities, Herculaneum and Pompei. Mount Etna, also a Stratovolcano, is the oldest volcano in the world at about 350,000 years old.

The Cinder Cone volcano is usually small, loose in form and built on the side of a larger volcano. The Shield or Dome Volcano is the largest type, shaped like a dome with long slopes, like Mauna Loa in Hawaii. The Super Volcano is the type that can change weather patterns on our planet. Its large magma chamber builds up over a long period of time before erupting. The last one blew 27,000 years ago but it is believed that about forty exist in a dormant stage.

A volcano is classified as either dormant, extinct or active. An active volcano is one that has erupted within the last 10,000 years. An extinct volcano has no lava supply in its magma chamber, and a volcano becomes dormant when a plate moves over the hotspot closing the magma chamber below. The magma needs to find a new way to surface so it creates a new volcano. The best example is Mauna Kea which helped form the Big Island of Hawaii. It last erupted in 2460 BC.

As a volcano begins to die, it no longer spews lava but can continue to emit steam. These are called fumaroles such as the many in famed Yellowstone National Park in Wyoming, USA, that awe thousands of tourists annually. One of the most spectacular fumarole areas in the world is in Alaska in Katmai National Park in an area called The Valley of Ten Thousand Smokes.

Geysers that emit clear hot water as well as mud volcanoes that emit boiling mud, are in the dying phase of activity. These are very common in Yellowstone National Park and the mysterious wilderness of the Nahanni Valley in Canada's Northwest Territories.

We will now study some eruptions.

2010 Eruption of Eyjafjallajökull Volcano in Iceland (Figures #23/24)

This is one of Iceland's smallest ice capped volcanoes but its eruption was highly significant because it caused enormous disruptions of air travel across the Atlantic Ocean and Europe for six days in April 2010 and other localized disruptions throughout Europe well into May. The eruption was not officially over until sometime in October of the same year only because ice had ceased to melt over the ice cap.

Some seismic activity was noticeable as early as December 2009, but nothing at a level to cause concern. By March it began ejecting some lava, but only about 2.5 kilometers (1.55 miles) into the air. Then on April 14, at about 7:00 am the explosive phase began but still only a VEI 4 compared to Mount St Helens in 1980 at VEI 5, and Mount Pinatubo in 1991 at VEI 6.

There are a couple of reasons why this eruption received so much attention. It occurred directly under the jet stream which just happened to be unusually stable at that time, carrying the fine glass-rich ash far and wide in a south-easterly direction over the Atlantic and blanketing Europe.

Also, the eruption occurred under 200 meters (660 feet) of glacial ice. The melting water flowed back into the erupting volcano increasing its explosive power. Since the lava cooled very quickly, it caused a cloud of glass-rich ash that is highly abrasive. By May 21 no further ash or lava was being emitted but it was not officially over until October 2010, although there is still enough activity to indicate it could erupt again.

The International Air Transport Association estimated that the total airline industry loss was around US $1.7 billion. It is estimated that airports, which had to close down completely in parts of Europe, lost over US$ 100 million. Over 100,000 flights were cancelled affecting approximately 10 million travellers.

The chart of the eruption makes a very interesting study: Observe the Gemini dual eruptions, the loaded twelfth house and the day of the New Moon. However, it does not tell us where the event will take place, which is why we need a framework such as the Geodetic Equivalent or Astro*Carto*Graphy®.

By observing stellar patterns forming, particularly eclipses in pairs, we can see an influence building, then determine where and what kind of event will take place. For instance, you would not predict a volcanic eruption where there is no volcano or the likelihood of one. Now see the eclipse pattern that sets it up.

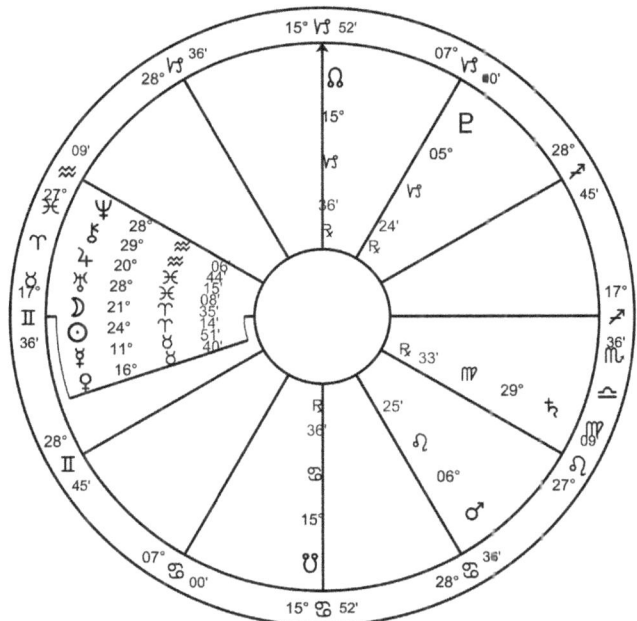

Figure #23
Eruption: April 14, 2010, 7:00 AM

Geodetic Astrology for Relocating and World Affairs

2010 ERUPTION OF EYJAFJALLAJÖKULL VOLCANO
April 14, 2010, 7:00 am Local Time
GEODETIC CUSPS FOR THE VOLCANO

Inner Wheel: TOTAL SOLAR (E) July 22, 2009 Duration 6'39" GMT 02:35:23 SS #136
Outer Wheel: ANNULAR SOLAR (E) Jan 15, 2010 Duration 11'07" GMT 7:06:39 SS #141

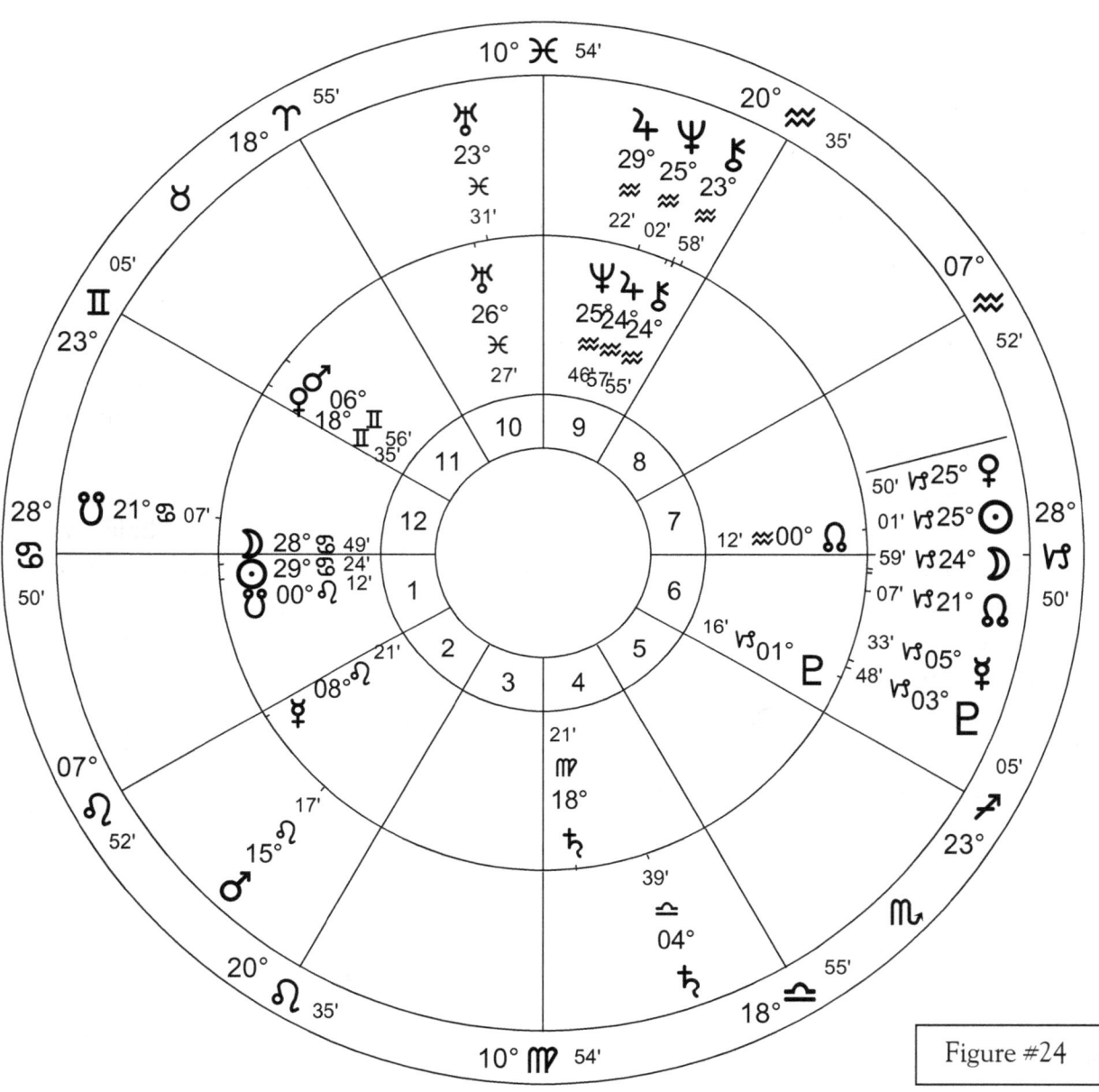

Figure #24

Note both eclipses are Total. They straddle the Asc/Desc.
Both eclipses are **exceptionally long in duration** for great strength.
New ☽ on day of eclipse 24:27 ♈ □ outer eclipse, Nodes and ♀ adding much influence
Transits: T ♇ exactly ☌ outer (E) ☿ ruler 12th and 4th houses
T ♄ 29:32 ♍ ℞ ✶ inner (E)

64

May 1980 Eruption of Mount St Helens Volcano USA VE1 5 (Figure #25)

The eruption of Mount St Helens in Washington State, USA, was a colossal spectacle of beauty and destruction that lasted for over two years, affecting many inhabitants at close range by the drifting blanket of ash that spread across the continent, and others through the watchful eye of the media.

Both solar eclipses in the pair directly prior to the eruption were central with duration periods of 6 minutes 03 seconds on August 22, 1979 and 4 minutes 08 seconds on February 16, 1980 creating stress in a vulnerable area. Astrologers should keep a careful eye on eclipses across Leo/Aquarius, particularly those with long durations. The pair in 2017/2018 warrant watching but they are not nearly as powerful as those in 1980. However sometimes it doesn't take much to set off an explosion or eruption in a weakened area if it is close to breaking.

For weeks prior to the first actual eruption of St Helens, the beautiful mountain dozed then quivered alternately, belching steam and brooding, while all the time its north side was swelling menacingly. The first notable action occurred on March 27, 1980 when steam and ash belched upwards for two miles. Then more brooding and quivering until the morning of May 18, 1980 when its fury broke loose. The mountain simply blew up a distance of 80,000 feet (24 km; 15 miles) into the sky triggering monstrous flooding, stinking mud flows and choking ash clouds, devastating the countryside for miles. It was the largest landslide in recorded history burying the Tourtle River 600 feet deep. Mudslides also reached the Columbia River fifty miles away.

The National Geographic magazine, January 1981, reported that the energy equalled "500 Hiroshimas" as it hurled over 400 million tons of debris into the air. The blast could be heard 200 miles away. In Yakima, Washington, 85 miles away, midnight darkness fell in mid-morning with winds blowing furiously and everything becoming encrusted with volcanic ash. In the first month after the eruption, that one city trucked away 600,000 tons of ash.

Fifty-seven people perished, thousands of animals were killed, and a vast landscape was reduced to wasteland. The damage was estimated at over a billion US dollars.

Prior to the main explosion on May 18, small earthquakes began registering in March, indicating that action was stirring below the volcano after 123 years of silence. On March 27, at 12:36 PM, PST, steam and ash rose in a column of about two miles. However, the first major and most spectacular eruption didn't occur until May 18, at 8:23 AM, PDT. It blew away about a cubic mile of its summit, lowering elevation by 1,300 and starting the immense land slide that buried the countryside. That was followed by powerful explosions that produced a column of ash and gas that rose over fifteen miles up into the sky. Smaller explosions continued throughout the summer and into the fall as well as throughout 1981 and 1982 when solar eclipses remained across Leo/Aquarius. The last major eruption occurred in May 1982.

Minor explosions continued into 1986. In 1999 the August 11 solar eclipse produced a powerful fixed Grand Square pattern putting Leo/Aquarius across the Geodetic seventh/first houses of Mount St. Helens. That is the eclipse that triggered the Anatolian Fault Line destroying Ismit, Turkey, on the other side of the planet with flipped cusps. (See Figure #19.)

Geodetic Astrology for Relocating and World Affairs

MOUNT ST HELENS VOLCANIC ERUPTION
May 18, 1980 8:32 AM PDT
GEODETIC CUSPS 46N12 122W11

Inner Wheel: ANNULAR SOLAR (E) Aug 22, 1979 Duration 6'03" GMT 17:21:48 SS #125
Outer Wheel: TOTAL SOLAR (E) Feb 16, 1980 Duration 4'08" GMT 8:53:11 SS# 130

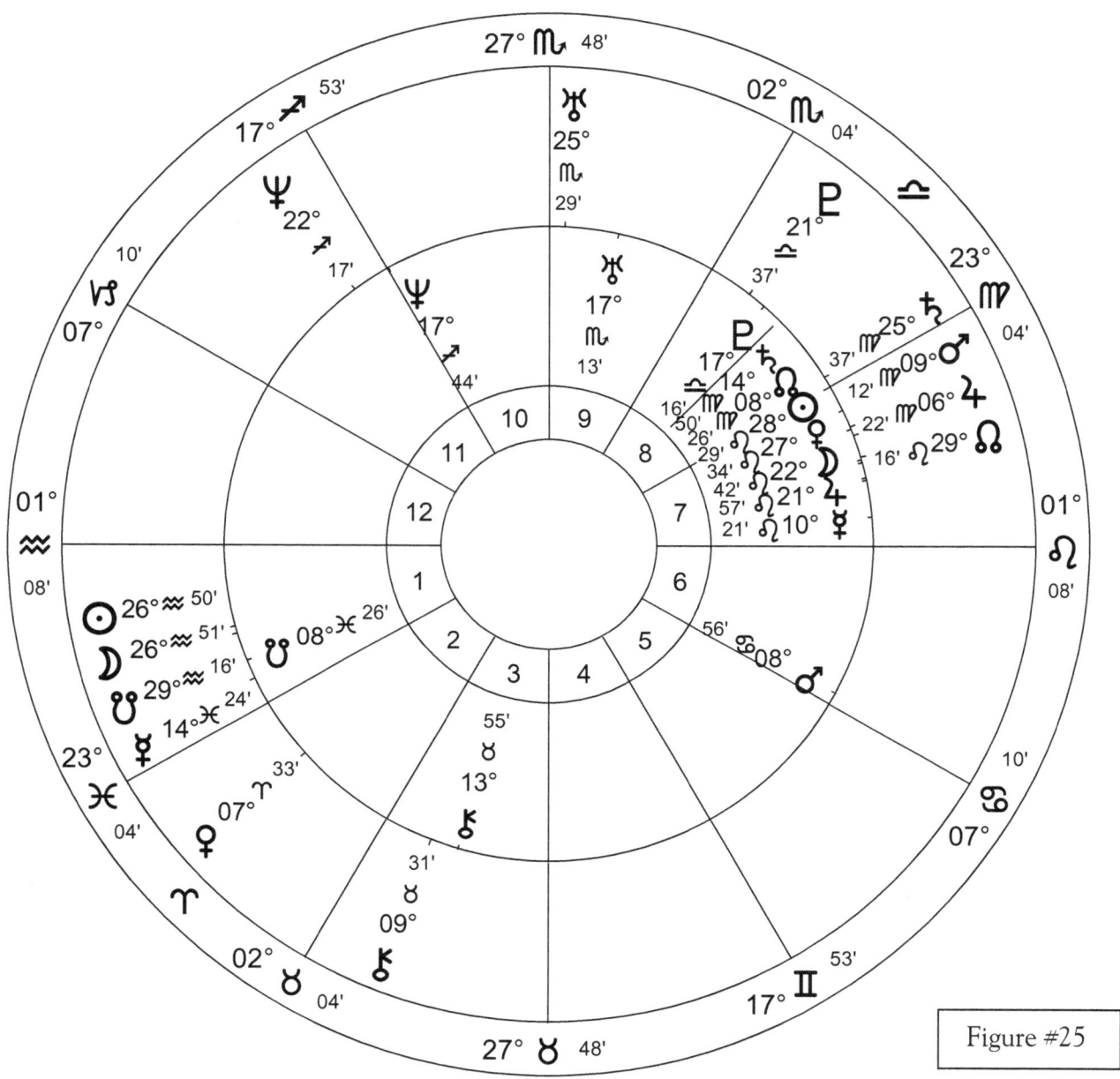

Figure #25

Eclipses on angles 1/7. Also note **long duration in minutes and seconds**
New ☽ 4 days prior to eruption May 14, 1980 at 23:50 ♉ △ 8th cusp
Transits: ☉ 27:41 ♉ ☌ IC
♀ 1:49 ♋ ☍ Asc (Out of Bounds at 27N10)
♃ 0:59 ♍ ☌ inner eclipse
♅ 23:23 ♏ ℞ ✶ 8th cusp

Declinations GE Asc 19S48, GE MC 19S40, ☽ Transit Decl 19N10

August 26–27, 1883 Eruption of Krakatoa VEI 6 (Fig #26)

One cannot talk about volcanoes without including Krakatoa. The eruption of Krakatoa in 1883 was one of the deadliest volcanic eruptions in modern times with a Volcanic Explosion Index of 6. Mount Saint Helens recorded a VEI of 5. The highest recorded index was April 10, 1815 when Mount Tambora erupted with a VEI force of 7. The year of 1816 was called, "The year without a summer". According to Wikipedia, the eruption of Mount Vesuvius, 79 AD, was not the highest index, probably about 5, yet it was the deadliest because it buried the cities of Herculaneum and Pompeii.

Krakatoa lies between Sumatra and Java in Indonesia. After having been inactive for nearly 200 years, the volcano began fuming, sputtering and quaking just after the eclipse of November 10, 1882 in Scorpio. By early May the following year, just a few days after the second eclipse of the pair occurred, it began belching fire, debris, and shaking violently. The transit of the Sun was opposing the place of the first eclipse, the Moon was in perigee, and Saturn was almost conjunct Pluto, with Neptune close by. Jupiter, now direct in motion, had arrived back at its position in the first eclipse chart. (See Figure #25.) For the next couple of months, sailors reported loud noises and clouds of ash high in the sky.

It waited until Mars and the Moon hit that powerful Jupiter position. The initial blast occurred at 12:53 PM on Sunday, August 26, sending debris 15 miles (24 km) into the sky. Seismologists believe that debris from this eruption probably plugged the cone, building pressure in the magma chamber until the following morning four massive explosions occurred that were heard in Australia about 2,800 miles (4,500 km) away. Can we possibly imagine how the noise would have sounded close by? The fourth and final explosion occurred at 10:41 AM sending debris 25 miles (40 km) upwards as the huge crater sank to the ocean floor creating 120 foot tidal waves. It continued to register for five days sending shock waves that reverberated seven times around the globe. It is estimated to have a force of 200 megatons of TNT. With about eleven cubic miles of debris flung into the sky, darkness fell as far as 275 miles (442 km) away. In the immediate area it remained dark for three days.

Tsunamis reached the shores of Mumbai, India, nearly 3,000 miles away, Colombo nearly 2,000 miles away and even to Cape Horn 5,000 miles away. In the United Kingdom 10,000 miles away, the convulsion of the air was very noticeable and small tidal waves reached the English Channel. Between the blast and the tsunamis, it is estimated that over 36,000 people perished.

For over two years afterwards, the dust remaining in the atmosphere created sunsets never since equalled. For months in Honolulu the unusual sunsets were green but throughout the rest of the world they were very vivid crimson. Even the Moon appeared to change color for a period of time due to changes in the earth's atmosphere.

Shortly after the "big bang" the crater rose out of the ocean again to reveal merely the stub of a cone. Over the years it has continued to build up. Krakatoa is very much alive today. Predictions are that it will erupt again one day with a force equal to that of 1883. It is in a very vulnerable spot on the Pacific Fire Circle.

The following year after the explosion, black rain fell in Ontario. The only attributable cause was the explosion of Krakatoa.

Geodetic Astrology for Relocating and World Affairs

KRAKATOA VOLCANIC ERUPTION
August 26-27, 1883
GEODETIC CUSPS 06N0607 105E25:23

Inner Wheel: ANNULAR SOLAR (E) Nov 10, 1882 Duration 6'14" GMT 23:22:24 SS #131
Outer Wheel: TOTAL SOLAR (E) May 6, 1883 Duration 5'58" GMT 21:53:53 SS #136

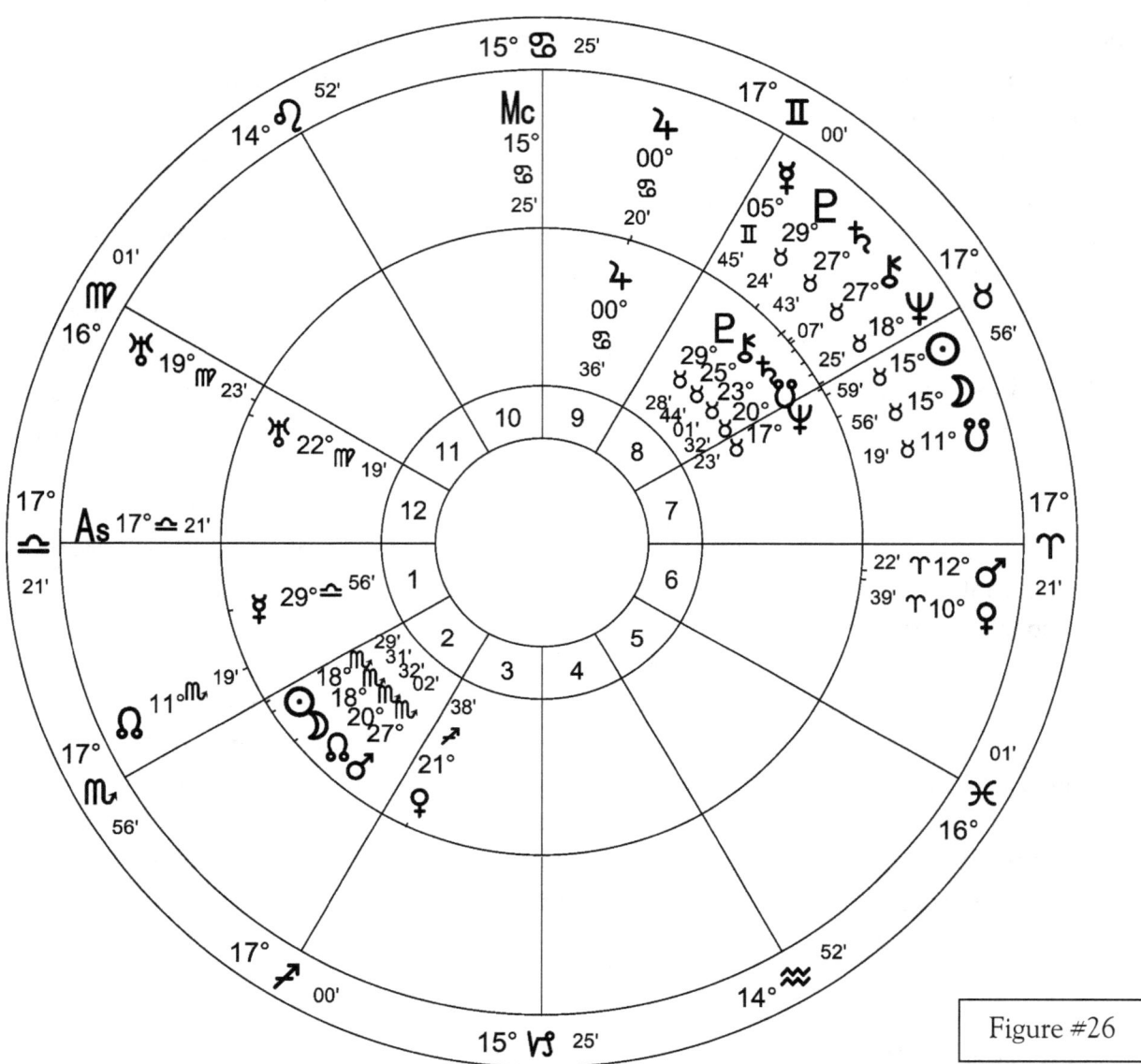

Figure #26

Eclipses across Asc/Desc Note **very long duration in minutes and seconds**
Previous New ☽ Aug 3rd, 10:21 ♌ in the 10th, square the Nodes (an ominous position)
Previous Full ☽ August 18, 25:12 ♒ in the 5th, □ ♂ of the 1st eclipse

3 planets transiting the 8th house as follows:
♆ 21:06 ♉ SR
♇ 1:12 ♊ SR
♄ 9:30 ♊
Path of May 6 eclipse arced across the South Pacific.

May 1902 Eruption of Mount Pelee, Martinique, No VE Index (Figure #27)

In late April 1902, Mount Pelee began showering the city of St. Pierre, five miles away, with fine ash. Then it began to hiss and fume causing deep concern. Some residents packed up and moved away. Torrential rains opened up from the heated atmosphere, flooding streams and countryside. More people packed up and shipped out, as natives from the country flocked into the city.

The rumbling of the mountain increased in intensity until it could no longer contain itself. At 7:50 AM, May 8, 1902, a mountain of flame shot upward just as the side of the mountain blew open hurling its fury on St. Pierre. Along with volcanic debris, the flames shot over the city like a giant blow torch, devouring it, capsizing boats in the harbour and hurling occupants into the boiling water. A great tidal wave was on its way to shores of the other islands.

About 30,000 people were killed immediately. Only four people in that whole city escaped the immediate hurricane of fire. One was a jailed convict who was housed in a poorly ventilated jail, but he was blinded and wandered around for weeks afterwards in a daze. The story has it that he later became a priest. A young girl hid in a cave and was later found unconscious in a boat out in the harbour.

On May 20, Pelee erupted again, this time killing about 2,000 people, mostly rescuers who had come to help the surviving islanders.

There is yet more to this frightening story. Close by on the following day Soufriere Volcano on the Island of St. Vincent erupted violently. It had been active for nine days. Deaths were reported up to 3,000.

On April 13, the Tacona Volcano in Guatemala erupted burying the city of Retalbuten under lava and volcanic debris. All through April and May, a series of earthquakes in Guatemala destroyed one major city and at least eighteen towns. Deaths were reported over 12,000. On October 24, Santa Maria Volcano, also in Guatemala, demolished dozens of villages, killing 6,000.

This sounds like some fabricated nightmare from a horror movie but it has been recorded by many sources, including the *New York Times*. It helps us understand the fury of nature that can be unleashed when cosmic energies line up to create undue pressure on our planet. Notice the duration of the lead eclipse at an extremely lengthy 11 minutes 01 seconds, with the other two eclipses merely partials at less than one minute.

In the eclipse chart preceding the eruption, Figure #27, we see three eclipses working together, two within thirty days of each other, and a pair in opposition. The first eclipse at 18:13 Scorpio forms a quincunx with the second eclipse at 17:43 Aries with an orb of only minutes. The third eclipse at 16:24 Taurus is in a close opposition with the first one. This is an enormously potent force.

The transits are not included because the third eclipse occurred the day before the eruption. Saturn had reached its station the day before, magnifying its effect, trine Mercury and quincunx Neptune. Saturn is in its dignity, which in disasters does not benefit but magnifies. Jupiter adds weight by being square to the final eclipse. Pluto was exactly on the mid-point of the Ascendant and the fourth house cusp. This set up could not wait any longer before it blew.

MOUNT PELEE VOLCANIC ERUPTION
May 8, 1902 7:50 AM
GEODETIC CUSPS ST. PIERRE, MARTINIQUE 14N45 61W10

ANNULAR SOLAR (E) Nov 11, 1901, Duration 11'01" GMT 07:28:21 SS #141
PARTIAL SOLAR (E) Apr 8, 1902, Mag. 0.064   GMT 14:05:02 SS #108
PARTIAL SOLAR (E) May 7, 1902, Mag. 0/859   GMT 22:34:15 SS #146

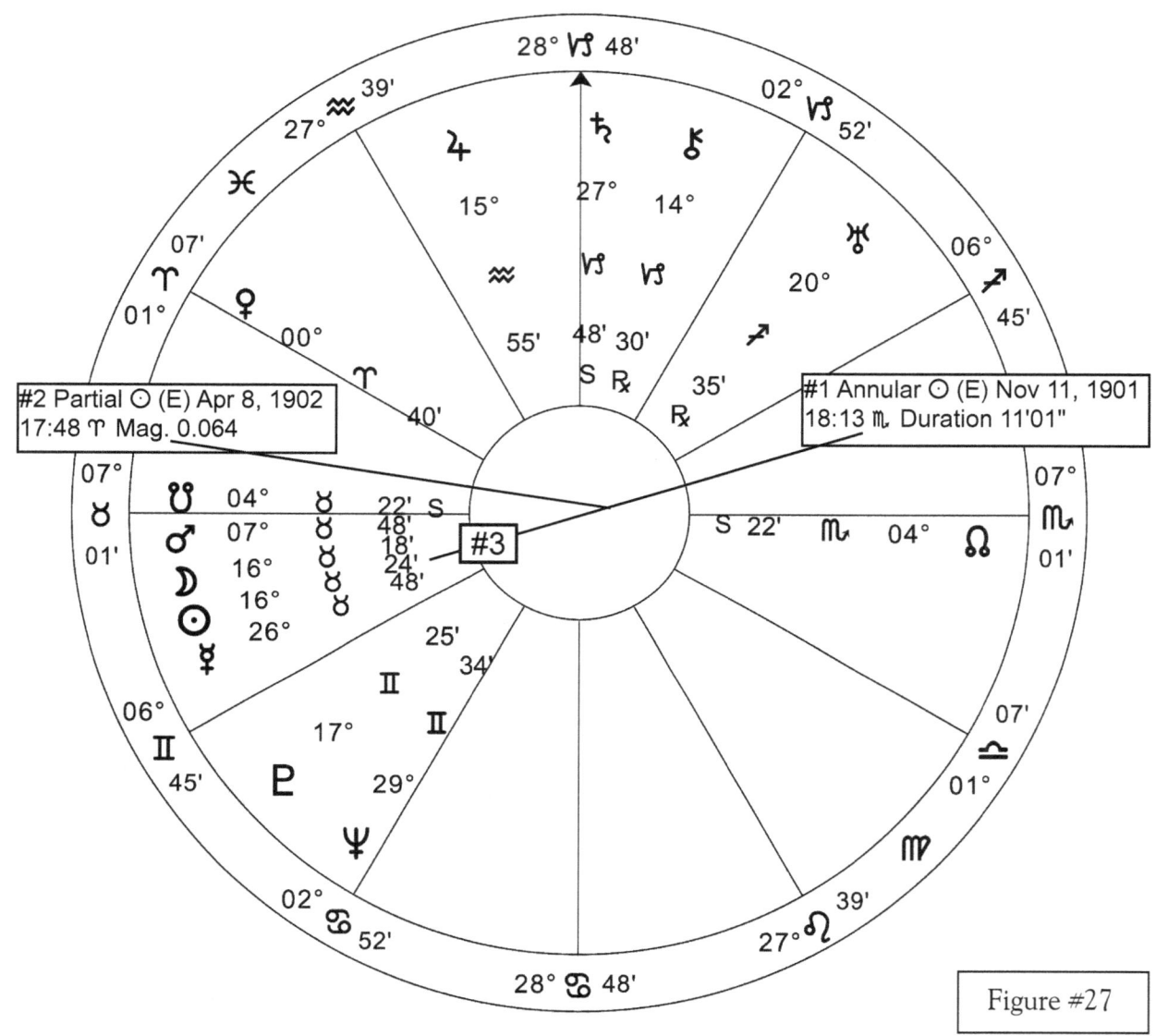

Figure #27

On occasion, two solar eclipses can occur within 30 degrees of each other as we see with eclipse #2 and #3 in April and May consecutively.
There is still an eclipse pair approximately six months apart between November 1901 and May 1902 across Scorpio/Taurus, across angles.

CHAPTER 5

Major Storms

As we follow the news, we realize that extraordinary storms happen everywhere in the world, but that certain areas are more vulnerable than others for specific types of storms due to various colliding wind movements and ocean currents. For instance, up through Central United States, along 90 degrees West longitude, is an area called Tornado Alley, named after the frequency of that type of storm. Hurricanes are a different classification of extreme weather, many of which generate off the west coast of Africa and build up steam crossing the Atlantic to enter the warmer water of the Caribbean and Gulf of Mexico.

There are many other kinds of storms such as snow storms, ice storms, tornadoes or wind storms, that can cause severe damage, if not just simple inconvenience. Waiting out a hail storm is usually relatively quick even though it can flatten crops. Basically, a storm is simply a disturbance of the environment. Severe weather can mean an unusual rise or fall in temperature such as the Alberta Clipper, a wind which blows down from the Arctic, gaining energy and influence as it crosses Canada, then lowering temperatures in the Eastern United States. Then there is the nor'easter (northeaster) that periodically slams into the upper east coast of the United States and Atlantic Canada. This is a combination of cold air from polar regions colliding with the warmer oceanic air from the Gulf Stream. It brings rain or snow, causes flooding, coastal erosion and hurricane force winds.

An explanation of storm types might be useful here: hurricanes, cyclones and typhoons are the same type of weather pattern, the only difference being where they occur. Hurricanes form across the Atlantic and Northeast Pacific. In the Northwest Pacific the same type of storm is called a typhoon, and in the South Pacific and Indian Ocean it is referred to as a cyclone. They are caused when ocean temperatures warm to the degree that clouds form from the evaporating water. Under certain conditions these clouds can gather together and begin circling or spinning due to the circular motion of the earth. Such a rotation can gain intensity and attract more clouds or it can slow down and become less threatening. Tornadoes are a bit different. They often appear with severe thunderstorms; winds shifting direction and rising in the atmosphere can meet downward shifting air creating a column of varying intensity.

All these storms produce vicious winds, incredibly high waves, torrential downpours, floods, and mud slides. They take human and animal life, and destroy crops and buildings. Hurricanes and cyclones are measured on a scale of 1 to 5 with 5 being the strongest. Fortunately most hurricanes do not reach that extreme intensity. Tornadoes are measured on the same scale as hurricanes although many usually measure lower.

One more distinguishable weather phenomena to mention is El Nino and its counterpart La Nina. Water in the equatorial region follows the pattern of the trade winds and El Nino is governed by a weakening of the trade winds. Normally these winds drive the surface water westward but when they lessen, the warmer water of the Western Pacific shifts eastward towards North and South America. La

Nina is a change in air pressure causing more intense winds, bringing cool weather to the same area. In fact, both are responsible for weather shifts throughout the entire world. A major El Nino event usually happens every three to seven years, forming in the late summer and lasting for several months at a time.

According to an index of El Nino and La Nina periods from the specialist website www.ggweather.com, the year 1987–1988 was an exceptionally high El Nino period causing torrential rain and flooding in areas such as eastern South America, Argentina and the Gulf of Mexico, as well as eastern parts of Africa encompassing various regions along the Indian Ocean.

This is part of the reason why Hurricane Gilbert in 1988 reached such a high intensity of 5 on the hurricane index. It swept across the Atlantic Ocean from the coast of Africa and smashed into the Caribbean. It continued westward into Cozumel, ran southward into Argentina, westward to the Yucatan Peninsula and into the interior of Mexico, then turned north through Texas and upward. It created extensive damage and claimed many lives between September 8 and 19.

It was the most devastating storm in hurricane history until 2005 when Wilma and Katrina marked out their journeys. Winds reached as high as 295 km/hr (183 mph), killing over 340 people. Damage was estimated at $7.1 billion without counting the economic loss from the tourist trade. Tourists were sent home and thousands cancelled their holidays due to damaged beaches and resorts. In the Yucatan Peninsula 83 ships were sunk.

The two previous solar eclipses at 29:32 Virgo and 27:29 Pisces are set on the Geodetic Wheel for Cozumel which is one of the areas where Gilbert made landfall. (Figure #29.) The Geodetic Ascendant of Cozumel is 4:22 Aries but by checking the Geodetic map we see that the westward direction of the hurricane shifts the Ascendant/Descendent axis into the late and middle part of Pisces/Virgo. This is where its intensity increased again to a level 5 hurricane. Various other eclipse observations add significance and power to this planetary energy, as follows:

The oppositions are unusually close with only an orb of 1'50".

The eclipses are within minutes of the Aries/Libra geodetic axis, often referred to as The World Axis.

There are multiple planets in Capricorn squaring the eclipses and forming a powerful Cardinal T-Square.

Both eclipses are central with longer than usual obscuration periods of nearly four minutes each.

Previous eclipses were moving in pairs across the Aries/Libra axis through 1986 and 1987 adding potency to the pair of signs and their pertinent locations on the Geodetic map.

There is one other condition that needs to be mentioned. When a planet's declination is north or south of the Celestial Equator and it is not in its regular zodiacal position, it has been called 'anomalous' by Heinreike Mayer, in the *NCGR Declination SIG Newsletter*, December 1999. Accordingly, it can cause many surprises including extreme weather conditions. It happens for longer than normal periods of time when a planet retrogrades over the Aries or Libra Equinox. Such is the case with Mars just prior and during this powerful storm.

Major Storms

Mars went into Aries on July 14, 1988. It went retrograde on August 26 at 11 Aries then went back into Pisces. It did not go direct until October 28, after Hurricane Gilbert. During this whole period while Mars was in early Aries, its declination should have shifted to north but it stayed south until November 18, well after the storm. That means its zodiacal position was out of sync with its declination for a period of four months. That is phenomenal because normally it should shift declination within a day or two. Figure #28 is a basic Declination Graph indicating when the declination of a planet should be north or south of the Celestial Equator according to its zodiacal position.

With such powerful forces of nature at work we look elsewhere on the Geodetic Map to find where Aries/Libra/Capricorn would be on angles or in angular houses. The influence of the eclipse patterns stays in place for several months waiting for a trigger in a vulnerable area.

We look to Bangladesh. The capital city, Dhaka, has a geographic longitude 90E21, latitude 23N2. That puts the strong eclipse T-Square previously studied on the geodetic angles, indicating that this area is singled out for a significant event. It could be political activity if there was unrest in the country, or one could logically be concerned about the weather because the country is governed by annual monsoon rains where floods happen every year. We might therefore expect excessive rain,

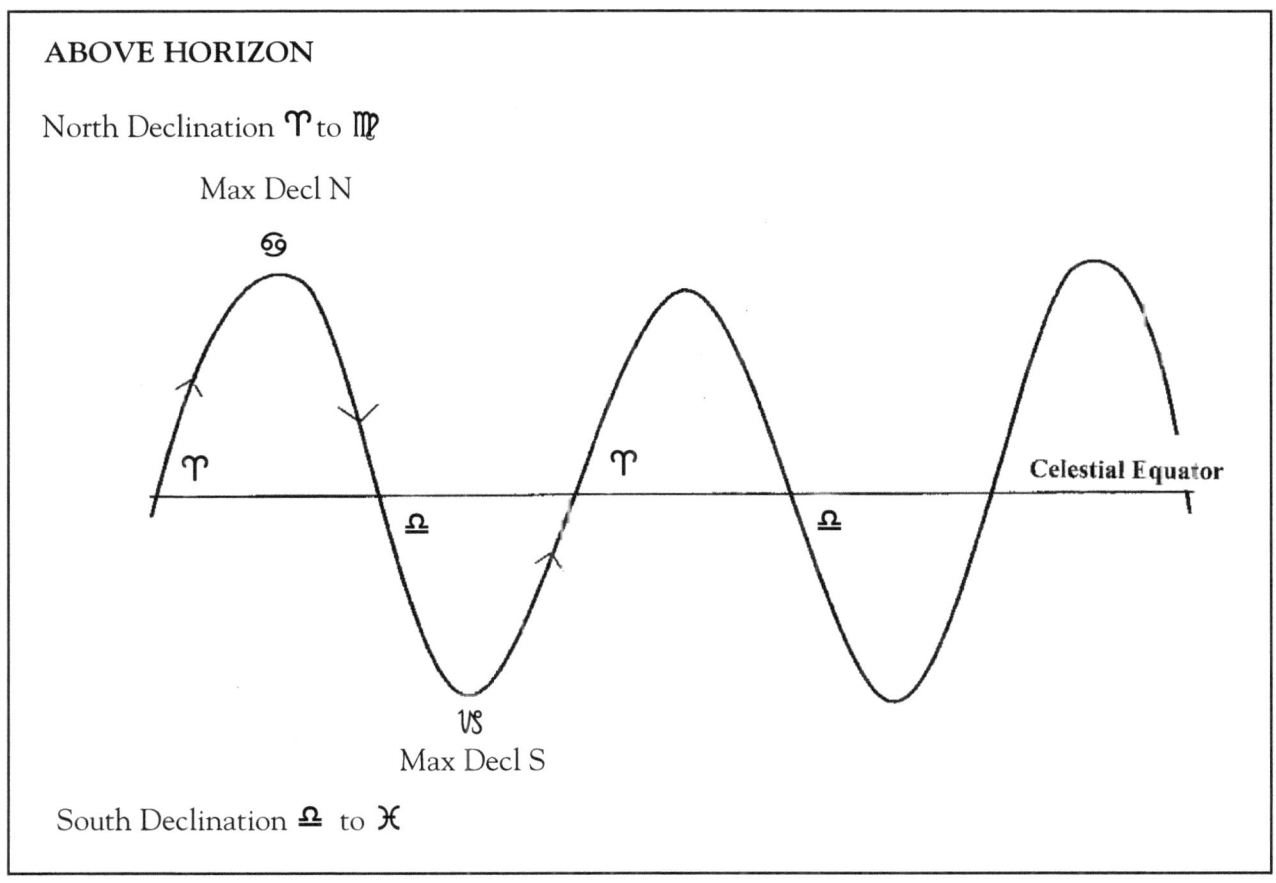

Figure #28 Basic Declination Graph

Geodetic Astrology for Relocating and World Affairs

HURRICANE GILBERT
September 8 - 19, 1988
GEODETIC CUSPS FOR LANDFALL AT COZUMEL, MEXICO

Inner Wheel: ANNULAR SOLAR (E) Sept 23 1987 Duration 3'49" GMT 3:11:26 SS #134
Outer Wheel: TOTAL SOLAR (E)   Mar 18, 1988 Duration 3'47" GMT 1:58:01 SS #139

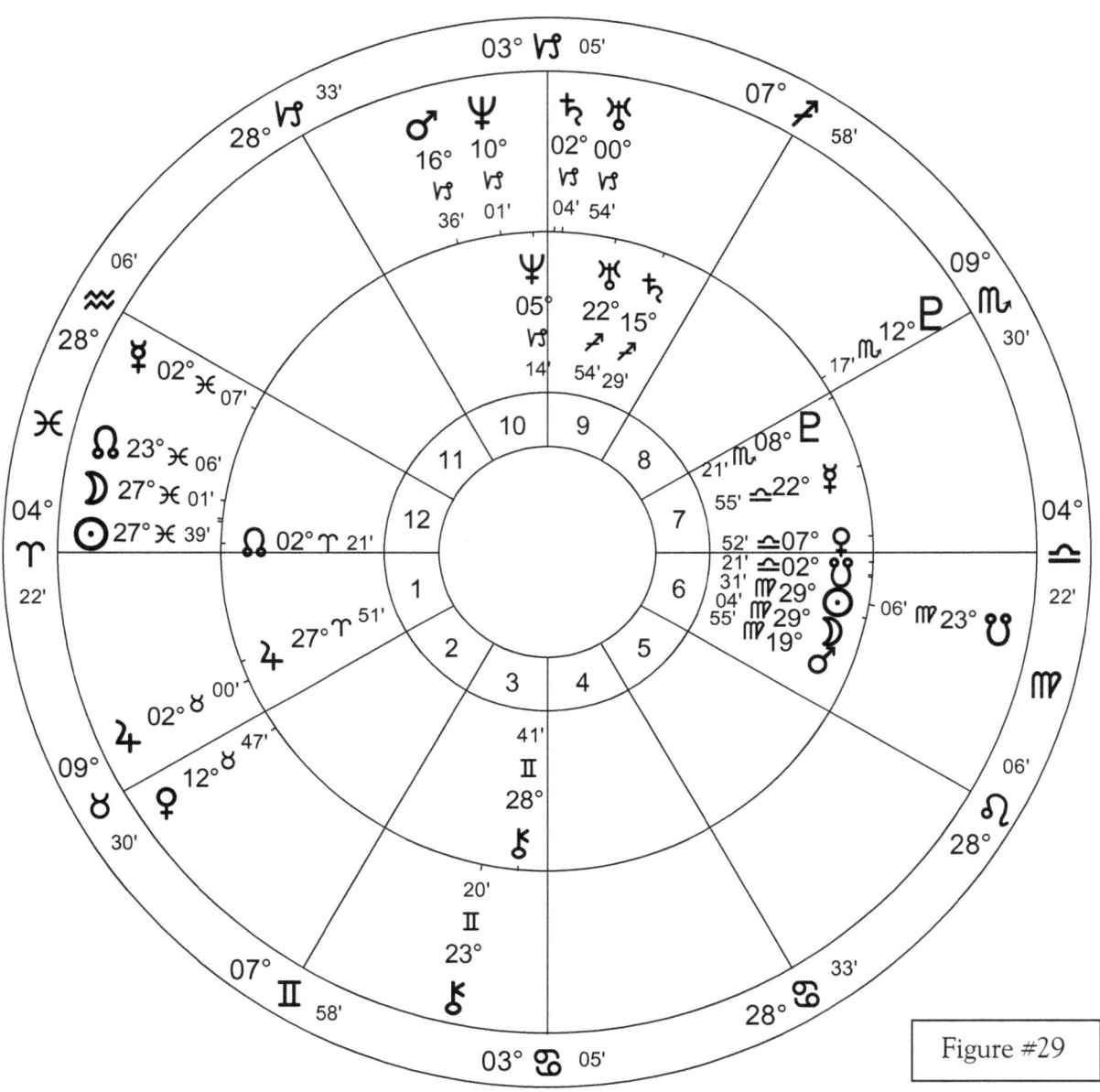

Figure #29

Strong consecutive solar eclipses, unusually close in opposition, are pictured here on the
Geodetic angles of the location where the hurricane hit land. The winds were exceptionally high
from crossing warm water. As Gilbert moved across the Gulf of Mexico onto land at the Yucatan Peninsula, the
Geodetic angles coincided precisely with the eclipse degrees in late Pisces and
the winds increased ferocity once again. Each time the hurricane reached land it slowed a little
then regained force over warm waters.

flooding and resulting destruction due to the strong El Nino year and the very strong T-Square eclipse pattern so close to all four of its angles.

One could check out the coordinates on a Geodetic map. The Figure #3 map is rather small so you may wish to run a larger Geodetic map on your computer. The full Geodetic wheel is shown here. (Figure # 30). During late summer of the 1988 El Nino season, the country suffered the worst monsoon flooding on record. River levels rose more than twenty feet, the highest in thirty years. About three-quarters of the country was under water including 40 per cent of the capital city. The death toll reached 2,000 with over 25 million left homeless and the entire rice crop was lost causing a great food shortage. The water contamination caused disease that affected more than 200,000 people, as reported by the daily news at the time. I recall vividly the pictures and front page newspaper articles reporting the enormous amount of devastation. The annual monsoon flooding is due to the country's location on the large eroding delta of the Ganges River and several other major rivers that flow through the countryside into the Bay of Bengal; the rivers swell in season from the melting snows on the Himalayan Mountains. This particular year, the monsoon rainfall was very high because of the exceptionally high El Nino level, as well as peak flows of major rivers from snow melting in the high country.

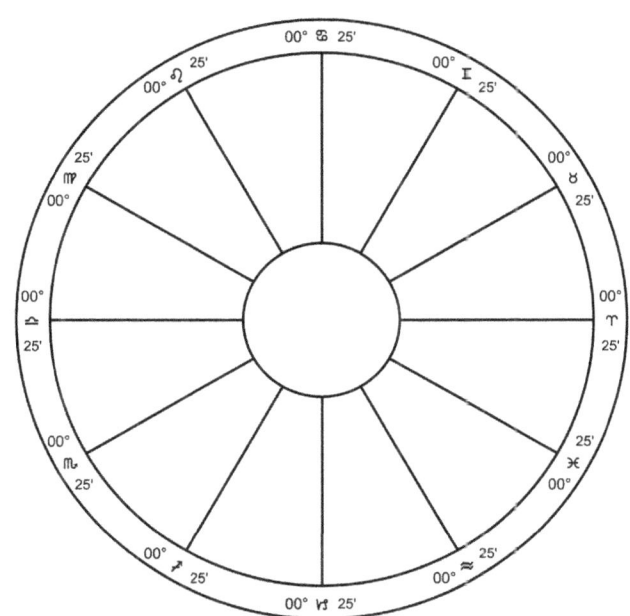

Figure # 30 Geodetic wheel for Dhaka

A sweep of a Geodetic map indicates many geographic areas affected by this intense influence. Here are a few:

June 27, 1988: A commuter train in Paris smashed into a stationary commuter train killing 56 people. (Late Pisces Geodetic Midheaven)

July 6, 1988: In the North Sea the worst oil rig disaster to date claimed 170 lives. (Late Pisces Geodetic Midheaven)

July 7, 1988: In Texas 14 people were killed when a store in Brownsville collapsed after a heavy rain. The Geodetic Ascendant is 18:48 Pisces, putting the eclipses across the angles.

July 8, 1988: In India more than 100 people were killed when a passenger train derailed while crossing a bridge and plunged into a river. (Late Virgo Midheaven.)

August 6, 1988: In India over 400 people travelling to a religious site were killed when a ferry overturned in the Ganges River.

August 21, 1988: India and Nepal, earthquake 6.5 on the Richter scale, causing floods and massive landslides. More than 900 were killed.

August 31, 1988: In Texas a Delta Air Lines jet crashed and caught fire shortly after takeoff killing 14 people. Geodetic Ascendant is 18:50 Pisces, putting the eclipses across the angles.

October 17–22, 1988: Hurricane Joan, Category 4, swept across the Atlantic Ocean, through Central America and onto the Pacific Ocean, leaving over 200 dead and costing $2 billion in damages.

October 19, 1988: In India an airlines jet landing at the Ahmadabad airport hit a tree and high-tension wires, and then exploded, killing 130 people on board. This Geodetic Ascendant is 12:42 Virgo putting the eclipses across the angles.

October 19, 1988: Near Gauhati, India, another plane crash in a driving rainstorm killed 34 on board. Ascendant is 01:21 Aries Geodetic Ascendant, putting eclipses across the angles.

November 6, 1988: In remote Yunnan Province, China, a 7.6 earthquake killed over 1,000 with 200,000 left homeless. (Cancer Midheaven and a late Virgo Ascendant)

November 19–23, 1988: In Thailand disastrous floods from torrential rain caused mudslides. About 1,000 people died and there was about $120 million in property losses. Soil erosion and deforestation increased flood damage and loss of lives.

December 7, 1988: Spitak, Armenia was struck by a 7.2 earthquake. Aftershocks continued for months. 50,000 people were killed and around 500,000 made homeless. A transport plane taking in supplies crashed killing all 78 aboard, and a second transport plane also crashed. This is one instance where the eclipses were not on the angles, but in the second/eighth house axis of death and destruction. The trigger was Pluto sitting exactly on the geodetic fourth house cusp on that day.

December 21, 1988: Lockerbie, Scotland, a Boeing 747 from Frankfurt to New York via London was completely destroyed by a terrorist bomb as it crashed near Lockerbie killing all 259 people on board and 11 people on the ground. The Midheaven of the crash site is right on the late degrees of Pisces.

There were many more worldwide instances over the months under this powerful pattern, but these examples are enough to show how severe patterns hit various global areas on the Geodetic map framework notably either 180 or 90 degrees apart in geographic longitude.

Hurricane Katrina

Hurricane Katrina originated over the Bahamas on August 23, 2005. By the following day it had intensified into a tropical storm as it headed towards Florida where it rained intensely in Miami and the Florida Keys; damage in this area was estimated at $523 million. As it crossed the warm waters of the Gulf of Mexico it intensified to a Category 5. By August 28 it had sustained winds of 175 mph (280 km/h) making it the fourth most intense Atlantic hurricane ever recorded at that time, though soon to be over shadowed. Katrina's damage was estimated at $108 billion.

The death toll was 1,833, mostly in New Orleans from flooding as levee systems failed, inundating 80 per cent of the city and countryside. Floodwaters lingered for weeks. Along the coastline of the State of Mississippi, 90 per cent of the towns flooded, with extensive damage as boats and barges were jammed into buildings, pushing houses inland.

Katrina's second landfall was Buras, Mississippi on August 29, where it maintained a Category 3 for considerable distance into Mississippi as it headed north. In Georgia at least eighteen tornadoes were formed in one day. Strong winds and rain continued upward through Tennessee towards the Great Lakes. As far north as Canada, remnants of Katrina brought excessive rainfall causing considerable flooding and damage.

In spite of projected figures, it is hard to evaluate the total cost. The hurricane destroyed or damaged at least thirty oil platforms and caused nine refineries to close, affecting oil production for many months. This resulted in an increase in oil prices throughout North America, to say nothing of the seven million gallons of leaked oil. Hundreds of thousands of people were left unemployed and over a million people were displaced and relocated throughout the United States. It caused the closure of sixteen National Wildlife Refuges. It took over a month to pump water out of New Orleans into a lake; the water contained poisons, raw sewage, heavy metals, toxic chemicals and oil.

We will examine the two preceding eclipse charts that correlated with Katrina and then add a stronger solar eclipse on October 3 preceding Hurricane Wilma that developed a couple of months later. Wilma started on October 16, 2005 and did not dissipate until October 30.

As you will see from information listed with Figure #31, the two eclipses before Katrina were not very strong, the first being only partial and the second being annular/total with an obscuration of 0 minutes 41 seconds. I suggest that the reason it correlated with such extreme destruction was because of the eclipses' close proximity of only 02:03 degrees in opposition across cardinal signs, keeping those degrees "hot" or active over the duration. They are also stimulating an area of extreme hurricane sensitivity on the Geodetic Map. In addition, the eclipse of April 8, 2005, had a geographic path that moved across the southern tip of Central America touching South America, very close to the storm area. This would seem to increase the intensity.

After Katrina dissipated and the clean-up was underway, the next solar eclipse occurred on October 3 at 10:19 Libra, following the same Aries/Libra eclipse axis. The eclipse was central in its geographic path, and its obscuration period of 4 minutes 31 seconds was higher than the two previous eclipses that correlated geodetically with Katrina. Accordingly, that kept this area on alert for further storm potentiality, which turned out to be Hurricane Wilma.

Geodetic Astrology for Relocating and World Affairs

HURRICANE KATRINA
August 23 - 31, 2005
GEODETIC CUSPS FOR LANDFALL AT BURAS, LOUISIANA

Inner Wheel: PARTIAL SOLAR (E) Oct 14 2004 Mag. 0.928 GMT 02:59:22 SS #124
Outer Wheel: TOTAL SOLAR (E) Apr 8 2005 Duration 0'42" GMT 20:35:50 SS #129

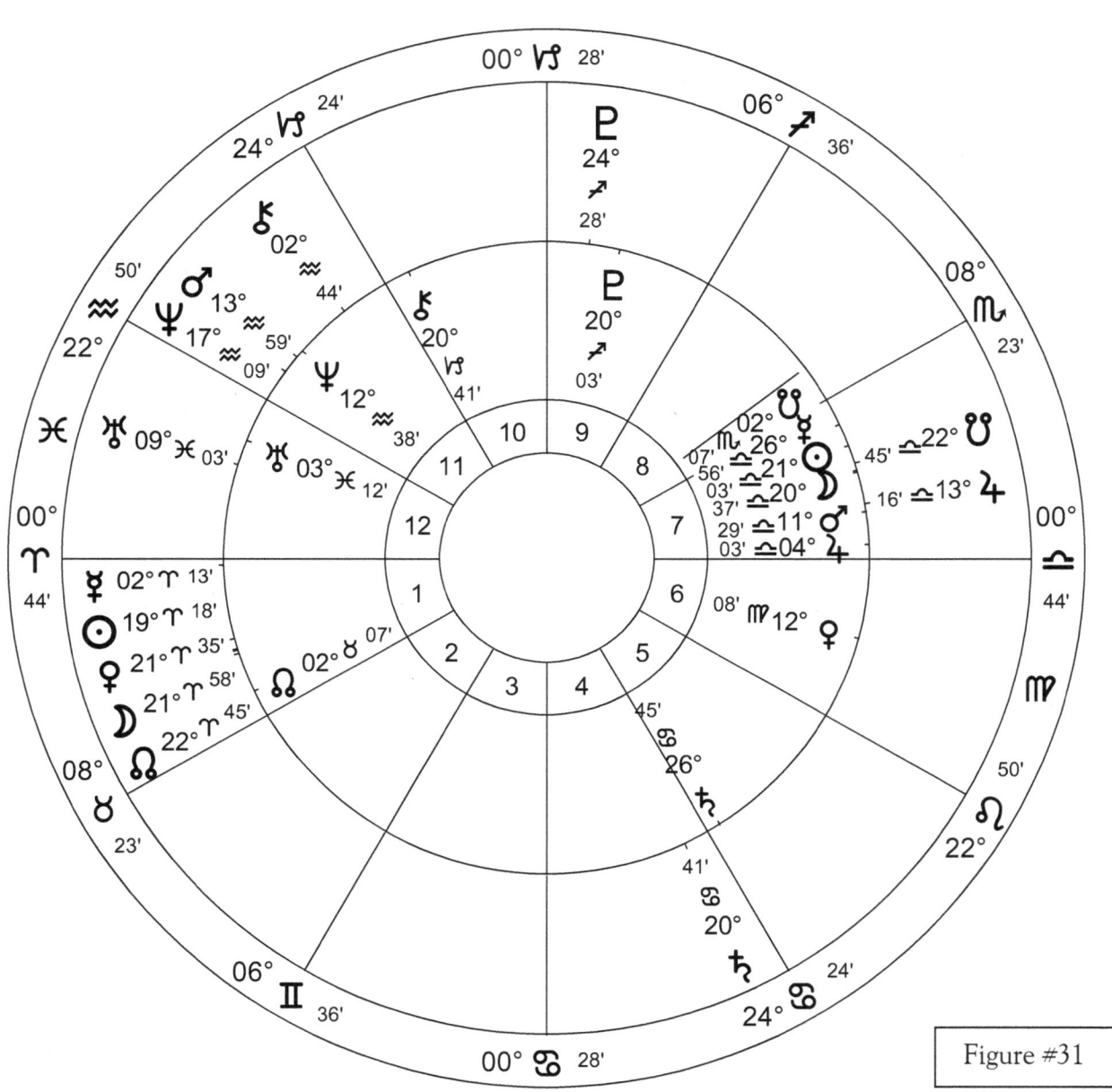

Figure #31

This is a potent pair of solar eclipses, being in opposition by only 02°03"
Previous New ☽ August 5, 2005 12:48 ♌ ☍ ♂ and ♆

Hurricane Wilma

On October 15, 2005 another tropical storm had its beginning in the Caribbean Sea near Jamaica where the Geodetic Ascendant is 18 degrees Aries, putting eclipses across the Ascendant and Descendant angles. Two days later it intensified into tropical storm Wilma. Shortly thereafter extreme intensification occurred and, in only twenty-four hours, Wilma became a Category 5 with winds of 185 mph (295 km/h). It tracked westward through the Caribbean Sea, causing extensive flooding and damage. Much of downtown Havana, Cuba, was swamped with six feet of water.

Wilma reached the Yucatan Peninsula on October 20, destroying much in its path, closing airports and stranding tourists in Cancun and Cozumel, areas that were still recovering from Hurricane Katrina. It battered the peninsula for twenty-four hours before it abruptly turned northward back into the Gulf of Mexico, making landfall again on the southern tip of Florida. From here it proceeded up the Atlantic coastline north to Nova Scotia, Canada, reducing its intensity to a tropical storm.

Wilma caused an estimated $29.1 billion in damages. In Florida alone the damage was estimated to be over $1 billion. About 62 people died, with at least six in Florida.

The year of 2005 broke several hurricane records in the Atlantic by being the most active and intense, replacing the previous record set by Katrina only a couple of months earlier. It set a new record for the number of Category 5 storms in one season. This should not be surprising when we observe the data we have collected to support eclipse patterns stimulating areas on the Geodetic map structure.

In order to investigate storms and geophysical activity it is helpful to print a collection of eclipse charts concurrently as a running ephemeris. Some astrology software programs will also print the eclipse paths. The following is a list of things to look for:

Partial or total eclipses in a consecutive pair that are less than 10 degrees in opposition.

Unusually long periods of obscurity, as in 2010 with two central eclipses with very long periods of obscurity at 11 minutes 07 seconds, and 5 minutes 20 seconds.

Planets conjunct either eclipse can increase its potency and hence predictability.

Transits that reach the midpoint of each eclipse.

Lunations as a trigger.

Observe if there are more than two solar eclipses in a single year.
From 1980 to 2020 there are only three years with four solar eclipses in the year, (1982, 2000, and 2011). There are only two years with three solar eclipses (2018 and 2019).

Five solar eclipses in a single year is very rare. In checking eclipses from 1700–2050 in *Planetary Phenomena*, I found only two years where there were five in one year, and that was in 1805 and 1935. The next will be in 2160.

Geodetic Astrology for Relocating and World Affairs

HURRICANE WILMA
October 15 - 25, 2005
GEODETIC CUSPS FOR COZUMEL

Inner Wheel: TOTAL SOLAR (E) Apr 8 2005 Duration 0'42" GMT 20:35:50 SS #129
Outer Wheel: ANNULAR SOLAR (E) Oct 3, 2005 Duration 4'31" GMT 20:31:46 SS #134

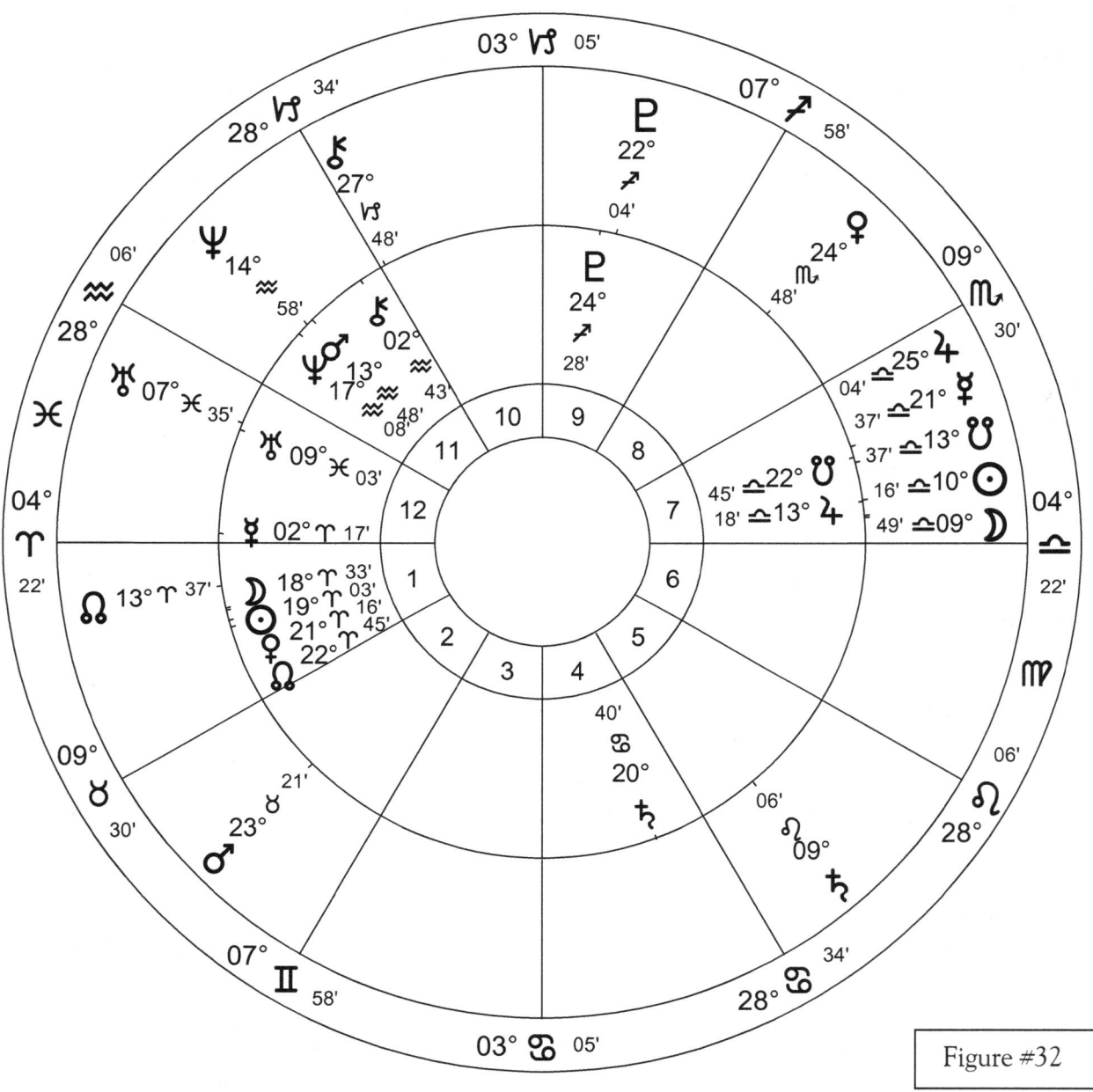

Figure #32

Hurricane Wilma was the most intense tropical storm ever recorded in the area. In fact, the year 2005 Atlantic hurricane season broke several records: It was the thirteenth hurricane, the fourth Category 5, and the second most destructive storm of the 2005 season.

Major Storms

Weather in Australia

As previously mentioned, wind shifts of El Nino and La Nina herald highly significant weather changes around the world. In Australia El Nino brings drier than normal conditions to eastern and northern regions, while La Nina brings unusually wet conditions to the same areas. This is opposite to the effect on South and North America and other regions previously mentioned.

For the two consecutive seasons of 2010 and 2011, La Nina had the strongest peaks ever recorded, a fact which should not surprise astrologers. When we check out the unusual strength and frequency of solar eclipses during those two years and look back on what actually manifested, we find that in this case its relativity to strong atmospheric shifts created extreme weather and geophysical activity. We will apply this to a couple of excessive storms in Australia.

Here is the list of solar eclipses for the years 2009–2011 taken from *Planetary Phenomena*. The year 2009 is included in order to gain our perspective because of the unusual number of eclipses with long periods of obscuration. That in itself is both uncommon and intense.

2009
January 26. Annular Solar (E) 06:30 Aquarius. Duration 07 minutes 54 seconds SS #131
July 22. Total Solar (E) 29:27 Cancer. Duration 06 minutes 39 seconds SS #136
(Here we see two solar eclipses back to back with unusually long periods of obscuration)

2010
January 15. Annular Solar (E) 25:01 Capricorn. Duration 11 minutes 07 seconds (Astounding) SS #141
July 11. Total Solar (E) 19:24 Cancer. Duration 5 minutes 20 seconds SS #146
(Eclipses continue with extraordinary periods of obscuration)

2011. Four Partial Solar (E) in one year
January 4. Partial Solar (E) 13:38 Capricorn. Mag. 0.858   SS #151
June 1. Partial Solar (E) 11:02 Gemini. Mag. 0.601   SS #118,
July 1. Partial Solar (E) 09:12 Cancer. Mag. 0.097 SS #156,
November 25. Partial Solar (E) 02:37 Sagittarius. Mag. 0.905 SS #123

Consideration must also be given to other powerful planetary influences of this time period such as the Cardinal Cross involving the powerful Uranus/Pluto square in Aries and Capricorn.

Perth, Australia: Hail Storm
South-Western Australia experienced a series of storms on March 21 and 22, 2010. One of the most intense cells hit Perth on Monday, March 22, from 3:30–5:00 pm making it the most expensive and damaging natural disaster in their history with damages estimated at $1.08 billion.

The storm included strong winds, a deluge of heavy rain, flash flooding, and enormous hail stones that measured up to 6 cm (2.4 in) in diameter, causing severe damage to many buildings, roofs,

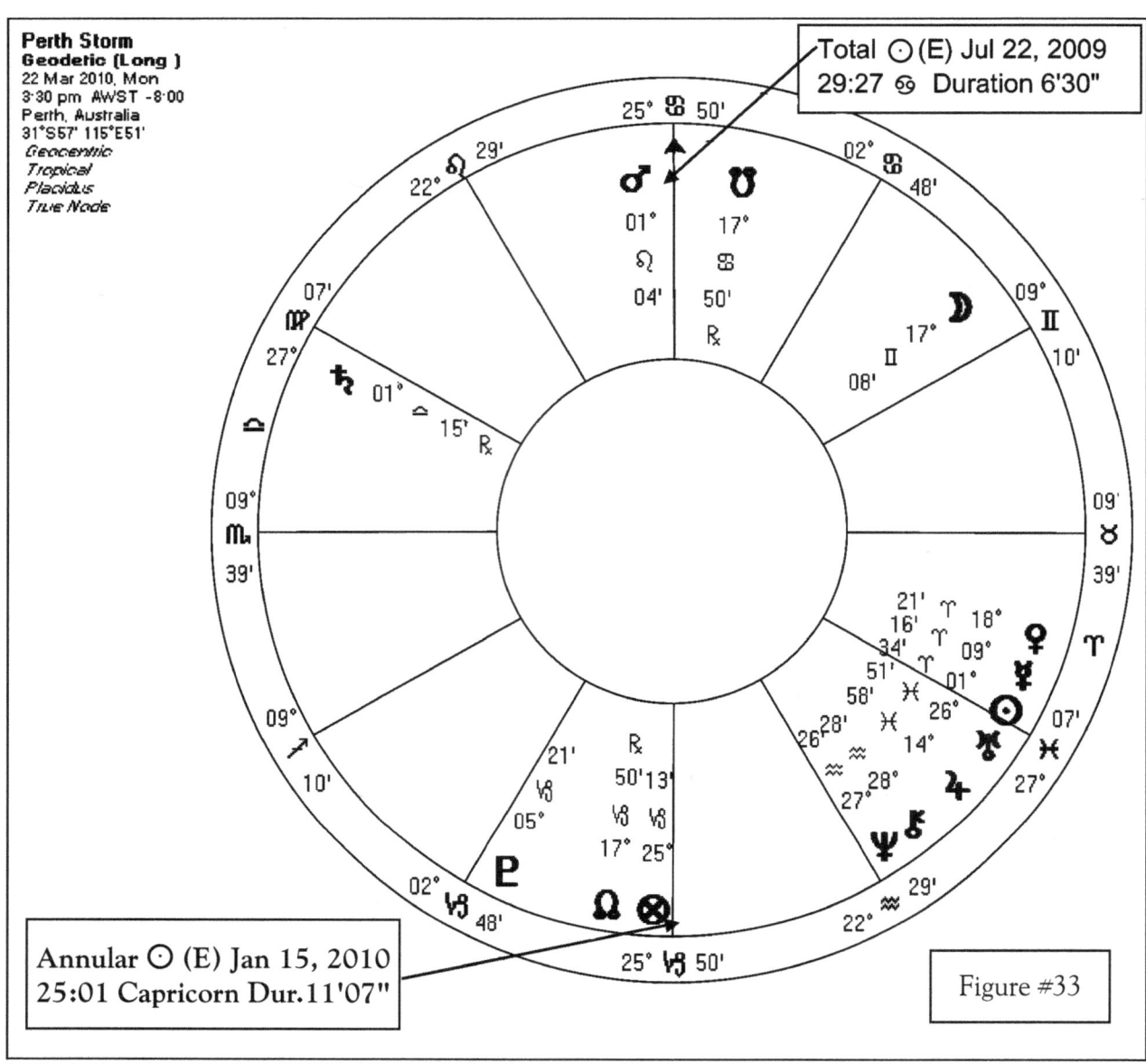

Figure #33

automobiles, and trees. The following chart shows the start of the storm transferred into the Geodetic cusps for Perth, as well as the preceding pair of eclipses. Notice that the eclipse directly preceding the storm is precisely on the Geodetic IC of Perth.

Cyclone Yasi

There was one other very dramatic storm episode under this powerful La Nina; Cyclone Yasi hit Queensland, Australia on February 2, 2011 as a Category 5. It originated near Fiji and intensified as it moved westward to Australia. The eclipses affecting this storm traverse houses two and eight on the full Geodetic chart. (Figure #34) The only application to an angle is Neptune on the IC. The reason the chart of the eclipse pair does not follow the angular positions is perhaps two-fold.

Major Storms

CYCLONE YASI
January 26 to February 3, 2011
GEODETIC CUSPS FOR LANDFALL NEAR INNISFAIL, AUSTRALIA

Inner Wheel: TOTAL SOLAR (E) July 11, 2010 Duration 05'20" GMT 19:33:37 SS #146
Outer Wheel: PARTIAL SOLAR (E) Jan 4, 2011 Mag. 0.858 GMT 8:50:42 SS #151

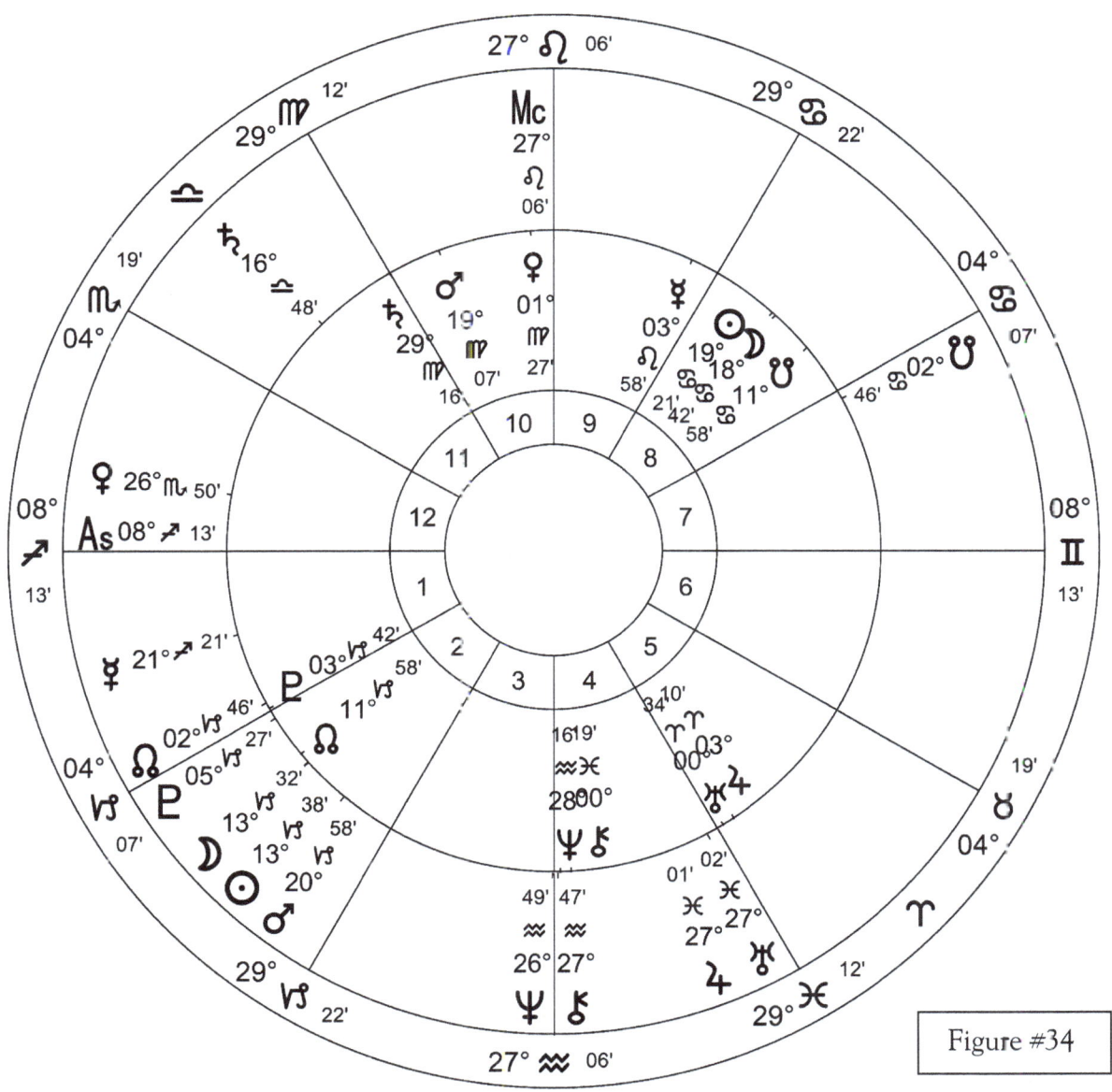

Figure #34

At the time of the storm, Saturn had retrograded back to its position in the previous eclipse at 17:09 ♎ forming a powerful T-square pattern. It is also the dispositor of the eclipse shortly before the storm.

New Moon 13:54 ♒ on the morning of the storm, ♐ 1st eclipse and ♑ the 2nd.

83

Firstly, these are the astrological houses of fatalities and extensive damage. Secondly, the origin of this powerful tropical cyclone near Fiji has the eclipses of Cancer/Capricorn well placed in the Ascendant/Descendant Geodetic angles. This could be an important clue in predicting the violent level of an upcoming storm moving towards land and destruction.

Cyclone Yasi hit the coastline of Queensland at 11:54 PM on February 3, 2011. The system was centered about 17N24 and 147E06, moving west. It struck land shortly after, near Innisfail and Cardwell.

First we need to take note of the two exceptionally powerful back-to-back eclipses in 2010, at 11 minutes 07 seconds and 5 minutes 20 seconds. They were close in opposition at an orb of 5:43. It then only took a partial eclipse in January to complete the amount of energy or force necessary to earmark this coastline for a powerful event. It was labelled the worst cyclone in Australia's history.

Prior to the storm hitting land, thousands were evacuated including patients in hospitals who were airlifted to safety. A storm surge reached 7 meters (23 feet) destroying structures along the coast and pushing far inland. The towns most severely affected were Tully, Mission Beach, Innisfail and Cardwell, although heavy rain extended far beyond these regions.

Devastation to the banana and sugar cane crops was extensive, as well as destruction of buildings and loss in tourist trade. The estimated cost was confirmed at AUD 2.03 billion in agriculture, mining and structures, and an estimated AUD 1 billion was lost in the tourism industry.

CHAPTER 6

Following the Daily News

As we have seen, predicting major geophysical disruptions and storms via the Geodetic Equivalent process is a viable framework or format worthy of our attention. It seems that certain stellar patterns can provide the kind of energy or pressure to cause a fault line to slip or a volcano to erupt. Stellar patterns can alter atmospheric pressure, change wind directions, change temperatures and release destructive fury on the land.

Political activity and societal shifts can also be followed and assumptions made when certain things are happening like existing stress, a breakdown of negotiations, or a dictator with political aspirations. We will look at the recent war in Iraq, as mundane astrologers followed its activity with careful attention, and study the terrorist attack on September 11, 2001, as well as other incidents in the news.

Other newsworthy events could come under the category of human error or equipment failure such as train wrecks, freeway pile-ups, or ships going aground and ferries sinking. One may ear-mark a geographic area for a special event but it is much more challenging to know if it will be a gunman in a school or shopping center venting his personal rage, or a large senior apartment complex catching fire causing havoc in the lives of many people.

Not every chart of a freeway pile-up has Uranus conveniently arranged in the third or ninth house square an eclipse in the Ascendant or Descendant, and neither does every chart of a big fire have Mars transiting an angle. Even if they did, pinpointing one single event in a large area that is under scrutiny needs some form of fine-tuning. Or perhaps it simply comes down to applying astrological patterns to specific events to determine if an accident or incident is in a high probability range. We may sometimes expect too much from our vigilance of planetary movements.

This shouldn't deter us from studying charts of these types of events however, because there is always something useful to learn. At the very least, the charts are interesting and could lead to inspiration and insight. In addition if the result managed to save a few lives it would be well worthwhile. In this chapter I will present and examine a variety of circumstances.

It will be evident that the eclipse axis is not always across the angles in these types of charts as was usually the case with earthquakes, volcanic eruptions and even the weather. However, the astrological houses involved are often specifically pertinent to the particular meaning of the event. As an example, in travel events, either the eclipse axis or other heavy planetary influences are most often across the third and ninth houses. There are exceptions. On the Geodetic cusps for the location of the sinking of the Titanic, the two preceding eclipses were across the sixth and twelfth houses, which is applicable to the situation; the sixth house indicating problems needing to be solved (why did it sink?), and the twelfth house indicating something hidden which is the submerged part of the iceberg. However, the event chart of when the Titanic set sail on its maiden voyage tells us a very explicit story. It is unfortunate that an event chart was not cast prior to the voyage.

The RMS Titanic: The Unsinkable Ship that Sank – April 14, 1912 at 11:40 pm

This magnificent and opulent luxury liner was publicized as the greatest ship ever to sail the high seas. She was 881.5 feet long, displaced approximately 46,300 tons, was stacked ten decks high, and could travel at the incredible rate of thirty knots per hour. On this voyage she was travelling twenty-three knots which was company policy on all maiden voyages.

The ship left Southampton at noon on April 10, 1912 (Figure #35). As we can see, it was an ominous time to start such a journey. She called at Cherbourg, France, then Queenstown, Ireland, before heading into the open sea for New York.

The ice flow that season was considerably heavier and further south than usual. To compensate, a more southerly course was laid, creating a false sense of security. Other ships that had sighted the unusually heavy quantity of ice were proceeding with extreme caution. The SS Californian cut her engines completely when darkness fell in order to drift rather than ram herself into an iceberg, but the Titanic was proceeding at its usual mid-Atlantic speed. By the time the iceberg was sighted about 400 feet ahead it was impossible to slow down or veer away. The entire weight of the fast moving ship struck a razor sharp underwater shelf and sliced a 300 foot gash in her side, exposing three large holds and two boiler rooms.

Below the main decks, immigrant steerage passengers were severely tossed about and had more reason to be alarmed than the luxury passengers up top, some of whom had even stepped out on deck to enjoy the adventure and to pick up chunks of ice that had been scattered about. It was only after the damage had been assessed that the general attitude became more serious, but the passengers were convinced there was no reason for panic. The Titanic was unsinkable! It was only after the deck began to tilt that the full realization of the impossible was possible.

There were about 2,224 people on board including passengers and crew, and only enough lifeboat seats for about 1,170 if the boats were filled to capacity, which some were not. Help from other ships could not arrive quickly enough, and for those who chose to jump, survival time in the frigid waters was minimal. About 1,500 perished, mostly men who remained on board to save space for the women and children, but some women chose to remain with their husbands. No one realized that the ship would go down so quickly and that help would not arrive in time.

The collision occurred at 11:40 pm. The coordinates are 50W14 and 41N46 for anyone wishing to look at that chart with its eclipse patterns. The ship sank at 2:20 the following morning.

There is yet another intriguing episode to this incredible drama which could be called a mystical prediction. Fourteen years earlier, in 1898, author Morgan Robertson published a novel entitled *The Titan*. It was the story of an unsinkable luxury liner carrying an elite passenger list, which collided with an iceberg in the Atlantic on her maiden voyage. In the story nearly everyone perished and the month was also April. The Titan did not have enough lifeboats to rescue the passengers, there only being twenty as to the Titanic's twenty-two. The fictitious liner was 800 feet long and the Titanic 882.5 feet long. This story was recorded in *The Darkest Hour* by Jay Robert Nash. See Bibliography.

Following the Daily News

EVENT CHART
TITANIC SET SAIL: April 10, 1912, 12:00 Noon from the port of Southampton, England

PREVIOUS ECLIPSES:

TOTAL SOLAR (E) April 28, 1911, 07♉30 Long duration 4'57" SS#127
  This eclipse is in the Midheaven, square Asc/Desc axis for greater emphasis.
TOTAL ANNULAR SOLAR (E) October 22, 1911, 27♎39 Long duration of 3'47" SS #132
  This eclipse is in the IC inconjunct Venus, ruler of the IC for great emphasis.

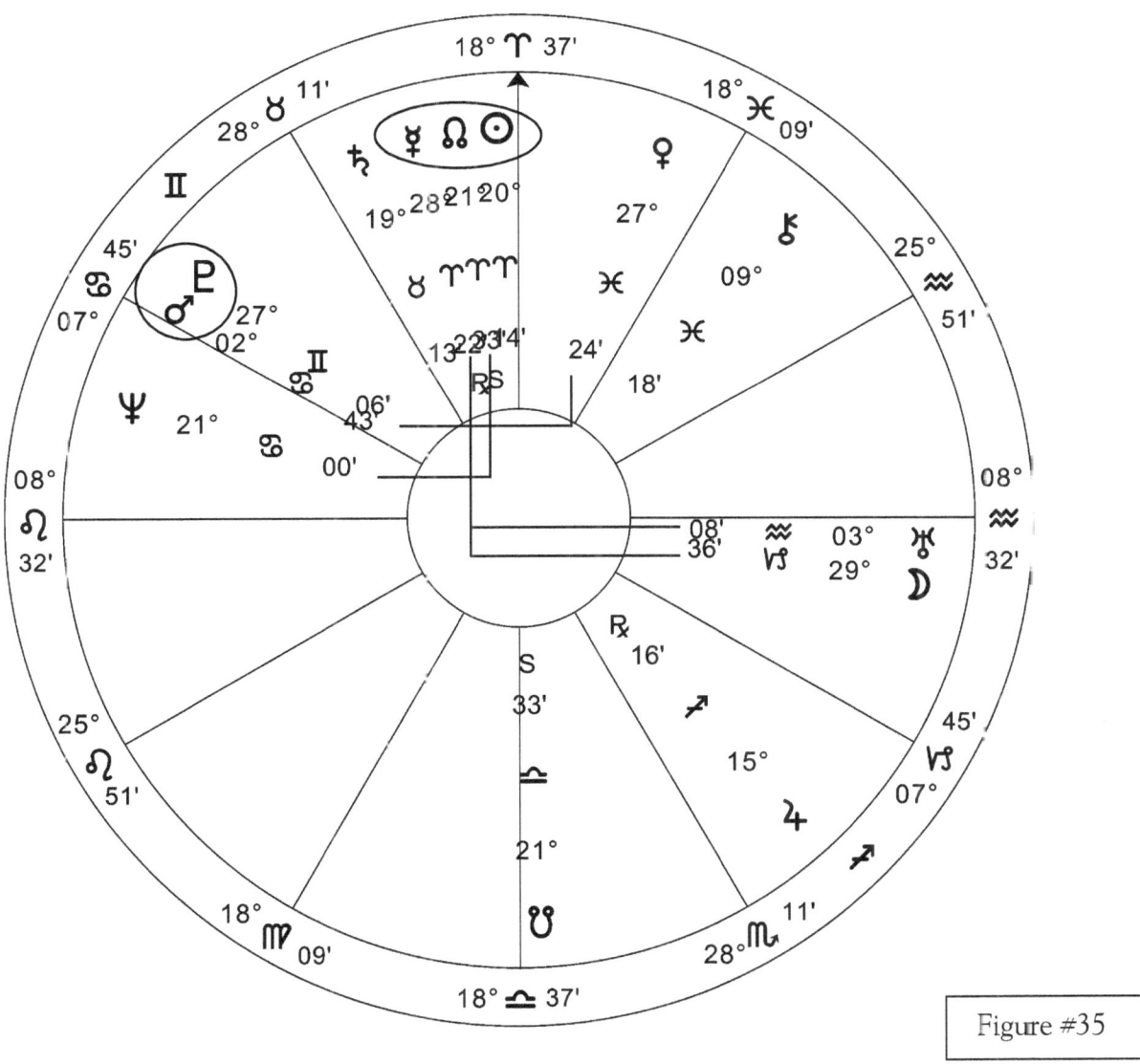

Figure #35

In addition to eclipse activity as noted above, there are several other factors making this trip a disaster: Moon Void of Course in detriment, square Sun/North Node that is square to Neptune of voyages. In an event chart, planets that square the Nodes are particularly ominous.

Operation Desert Storm (Figure #36)

The original intention of this war was to expel Iraqi troops from their occupational takeover of Kuwait. It was sanctioned by the United Nations and became a coalition led by the United States. The Iraqi troops were expelled and pushed back to within 150 miles (240 km) of Bagdad. On February 28, 1991, President Bush declared a ceasefire and the liberation of Kuwait. Here we see the Geodetic charts for the start of the war for both Bagdad and Washington. It is interesting to note that the eclipse pair directly before the war started was across the sixth and twelfth houses of Bagdad and across the MC/IC axis in the Washington Geodetic Chart. It is surely because, in this instance, the United States was the aggressor by leading the attack. The two eclipses are central and of long duration. One eclipse was two days prior to the start of the war, conjunct Saturn. Note Uranus/Neptune Great Conjunction and multiple Capricorn energy.

OPERATION DESERT STORM
January 17, 1991 – First missiles crossed the border into Iraq at 2:20 AM
GEODETIC CUSPS: Washington D.C. and Bagdad, Iraq

TWO PREVIOUS ECLIPSES:
TOTAL SOLAR (E) July 22, 1990   29:04 ♋ Duration 2'33" SS #126
ANNULAR SOLAR (E) January 15, 1991   25:20 ♑ Duration 7'36" SS #131

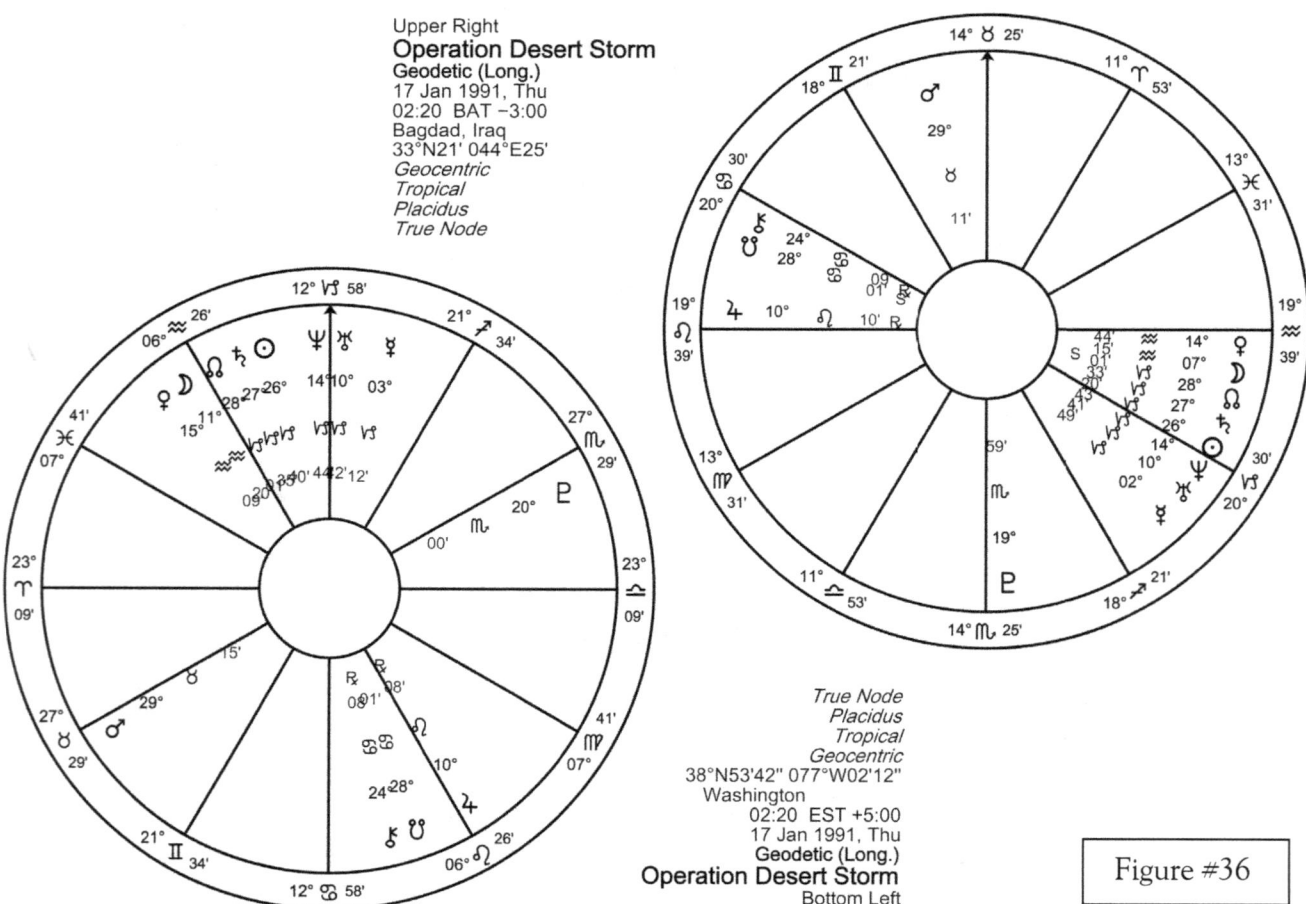

Figure #36

Terrorist Attack of 9/11

It is mandatory that a book such as this should include an astrological study of the terrorist attack on the Twin Towers in New York on September 11, 2001, now known simply as 9/11. As everyone knows, there were four different coordinated attacks that day:

American Airlines Flight #11 crashed into the North Twin Tower
United Airline Flight #175 crashed into the South Twin Tower
American Airlines Flight #77 crashed into the Pentagon
United Airlines Flight #93, targeted at Washington crashed into a field in Pennsylvania

A total of 2,996 people died in this vicious attack, including 227 civilians and the 19 hijackers who were aboard the planes. Within a couple of hours the two buildings of the Twin Towers collapsed spreading debris and causing fires that damaged many surrounding structures.

The world spun into shock at such a blatant attack. All flights going into the United States were grounded for several days. A friend from Florida, returning from London, was grounded in Newfoundland where many were housed for several days on cots in gymnasiums and other resources. I was told they were graciously taken care of by the Canadian people who were also in deep shock and grief. I had a speaking engagement in Boston that had been booked a year before, and I was coincidentally already booked on the first flight out of Canada that was allowed into American territory after the attack. When I arrived in Toronto to change flights, the airport was eerily vacant and quiet, with soldiers patrolling carrying machine guns. It was the same atmosphere when I arrived in Boston and walked through the airport. Flying has never been the same since, with strict security measures now at all airports worldwide. In fact there is always a sense of insecurity lurking inside our hearts and minds every time we go into a large public area.

Blame for the attack was laid on al-Qaeda terrorists led and financed by Osama bin Laden. Previously, in 1998, Osama bin Laden had proclaimed a holy war against the United States, calling for the killing of American civilians. His reasons were many as is often the case with this type of fundamentalism.

After 9/11, the US launched a War on Terrorism going into Afghanistan where, it was believed, the Taliban were harbouring al-Quaeda fundamentalists and bin Laden in the rugged mountain regions. Bin Laden was finally captured and killed in May 2011.

The first study shows the attack chart in the Geodetic cusps of New York with its Midheaven at 15:59 Capricorn. Boston, the location of the first hijacked plane, has a close Geodetic Midheaven at 18:56 Capricorn; Washington's Geodetic Midheaven is 12:57 Capricorn.

The four solar and lunar eclipses running from December 25, 2000 to July 5, 2001, preceding the attack, all hover around the ninth and tenth houses, with one exception. The ninth house represents ideologies, beliefs and multi-cultural activities. The 10th of course governs one's position in the world, reputation and fate. The one eclipse exception is the total solar eclipse of June 21, 2001 just before the attack, at 00:11 Cancer. It had a long obscuration period of 4 minutes 50 seconds adding to its strength and influence. It is in close opposition to the partial solar eclipse of December 25, 2000 at 04:15 Capricorn. Then we observed the power struggle of Saturn opposition Pluto across the second and eighth houses, indicating death and destruction.

TERRORIST ATTACK, September 11, 2001, 8:46 AM
GEODETIC CUSPS: NEW YORK

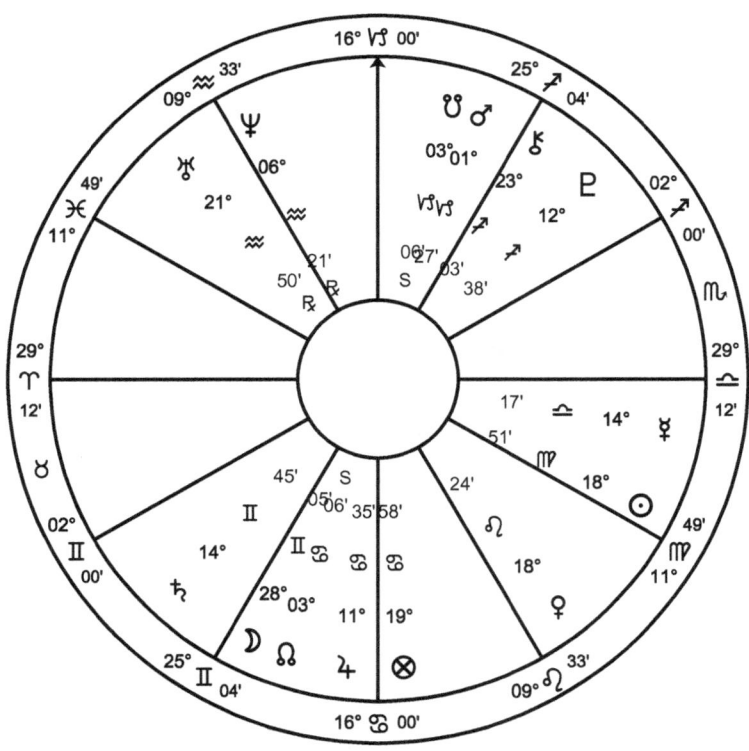

Dec. 25, 2000 Partial ☉ (E)
04:13 ♑ Mag. 0.723

Jan 9, 2001 Total ☽ (E)
19:28 ♋

June 21, 2001 Total ☉ (E)
00:11 ♋ Dur. 04'56"
July 5, 2001 Partial ☽ (E)
13:34 ♑

Aftermath:
Annular ☉ (E) after 9/11
Dec 14, 2001 3'53"
22:56 ♐

Figure #37

In this connection there is one other interesting thought to consider, and that is the chart of the Great Mutation of Jupiter/Saturn progressed forward to September 11, 2001.

The Jupiter/Saturn cycle occurs every twenty years, dividing its influence by elements. Charles Harvey calls these conjunctions, "The Great Chronocrators or rulers of history." It is the force that allows ideas to develop and flourish and become grounded in the practical world. The conjunctions occur in the same element for 200–240 years then change or mutate into a new sign, although they revert back for one more conjunction before staying in the new element. It is suggested that each element puts its stamp or influence on the decades ahead. Accordingly, when the conjunction returns to a Fire sign it is a Great Mutation, as it begins mutating through the elements again. But this is actually a misconception.

At an Astrological Association conference in York, England in 2002, Robert Hand mentioned that the ancient Persian astrologer, Abdul Mashar, said the Great Mutation is when it goes into the first term or bound of the first sign, Aries. A sign is divided into five terms or bounds of six degrees each, hence there would only be a Great Mutation when the conjunction occurs in the first six degrees of Aries. In *Tables of Planetary Phenomena* by Neil Michelson, under Outer Planet Conjunctions, data gives May 21, 1702, 8:57 PM as the conjunction occurring at 6:36 Aries.

The Great Mutation is said to set the world's pace for years ahead whereas each regular conjunction sets the course of mundane affairs for twenty years, as well as its division by elements.

Figure #38 shows the chart of the Great Mutation, progressed forward to September 11, 2001 relocated to Geodetic Cusps, New York. Note that the progressed date is March 16, 1703.

THE GREAT MUTATION (Figure #38)
Progressed to September 11, 2001
GEODETIC CUSPS: New York

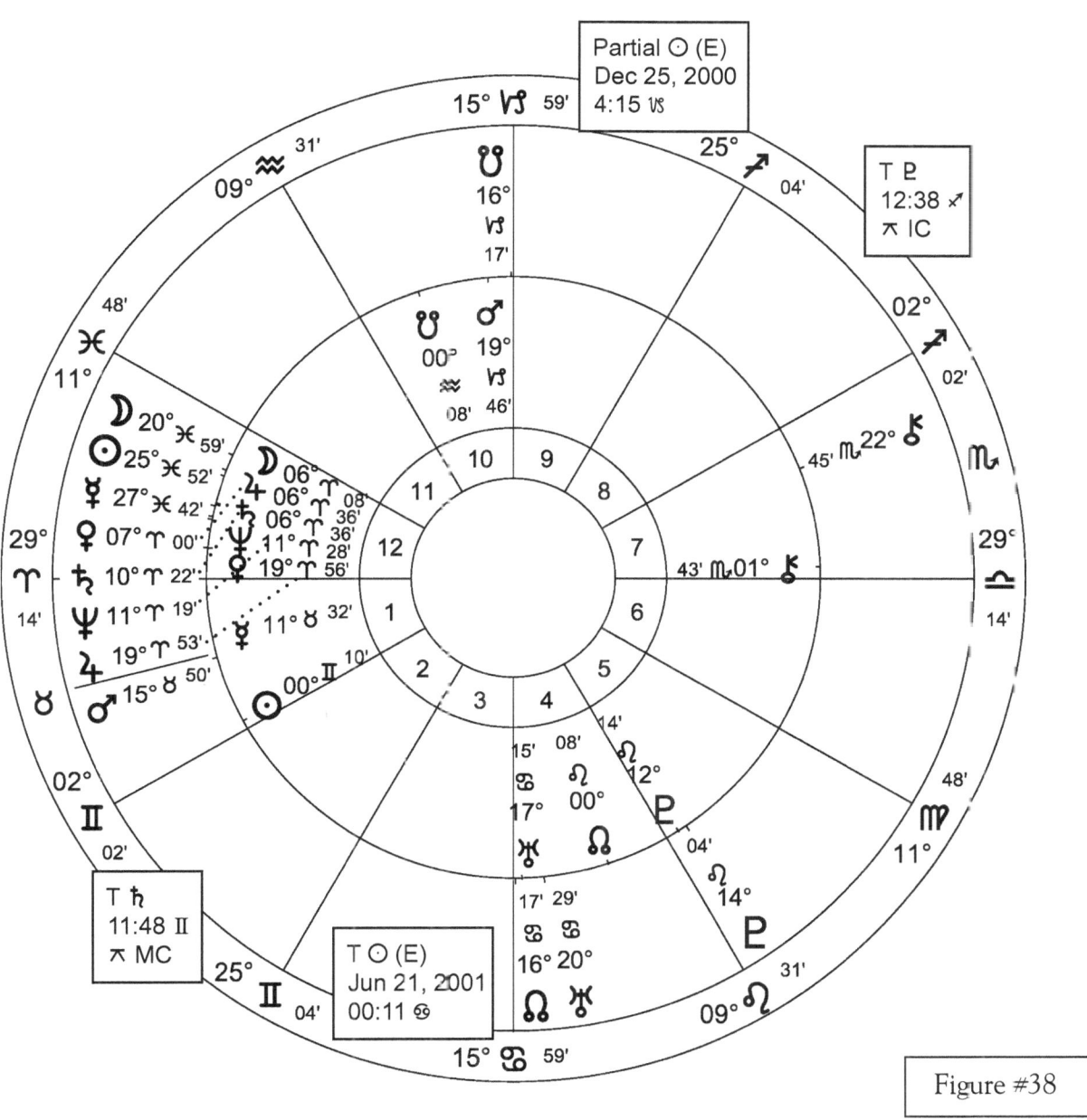

Figure #38

Significant aspects as follows:
Two solar eclipses prior to 9/11 across houses 3/9 □ ♈ progressions in 12th.
3/9 are houses of ideas, ideologies, beliefs, multiculturism, religious views, which were all part of the story.
Progressed Nodal axis across MC/IC conjunct ♅: This is an ominous position portending disaster.
Transiting ♄/♇ ☍ across houses 2/8 indicating loss and imbalance of power.
Progressed ☽ 25:35 ♓ square houses 3/9.

Geodetic Astrology for Relocating and World Affairs

Invasion of Iraq Figure (Figure #39)

This invasion was a coalition led by the United States, including Great Britain, Australia, and Poland. The mission was to disarm Iraq from weapons of mass destruction, depose Saddam Hussein in order to eliminate his support for terrorism, and to free the people of Iraq. With its arsenal of weapons, Iraq was deemed a threat to world peace. The invasion started with a series of air strikes against government and military installations, which were then followed up by ground forces.

PREVIOUS ECLIPSES:
   ANNULAR SOLAR (E) June 10, 2002, 19♊54, 0 minutes 22 seconds, SS #137, ☊
   TOTAL SOLAR (E) December 4, 2002, 11♐58, 2 minutes 4 seconds, SS #142, ☋
   Lunar eclipses of 2002 including 27♑39 and 03♑02

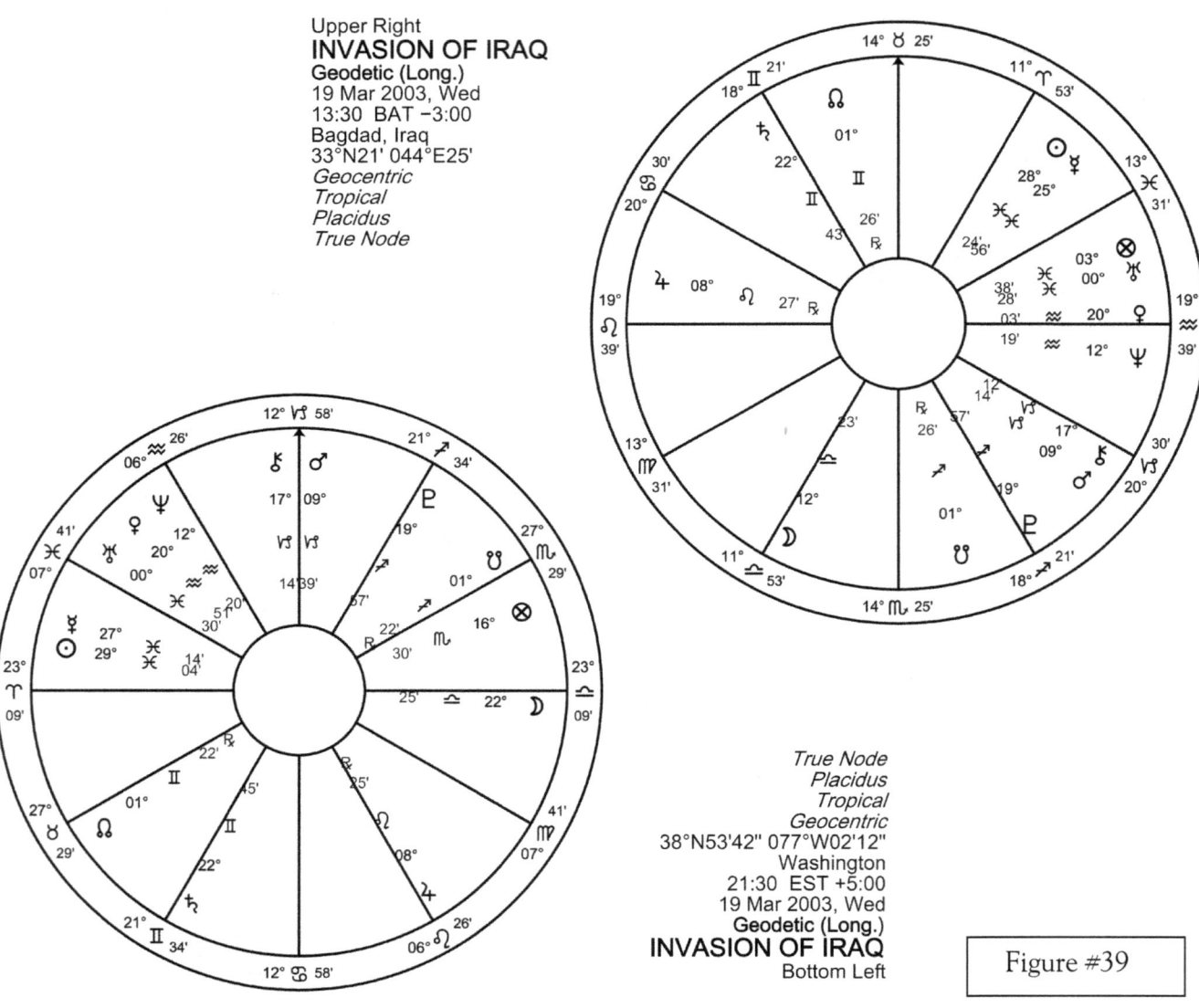

We can readily see the eclipse influences across houses 2/8 in the Geodetic chart for Washington,
♂ on the Midheaven, and ☽ on the 7th house cusp of open enemies.
The eclipses fall across the angles, with the ♄/♇ opposition close by.
In the Geodetic chart for Bagdad the eclipses fall across the MC/IC axis.

The Rwanda Genocide: April 7–July 15, 1994 (Figure #40)

This vicious slaughter lasted approximately 100 days killing an estimated 500,000–1,000,000 Tutsi and moderate Hutu people by the Hutu majority members. It constituted about twenty per cent of the total population of the country and about seventy per cent of the men. It was a political movement in the extreme by those who were in power in the government of the country. Those doing the killing were members of the Rwandan army, the National Police, government-backed militia, and civilians. The following chart is set for noon on the day the massacre started, in the Geodetic cusps for the capital city Kigali.

The eclipse prior to the event:
   Partial ☉ (E) Nov 13, 1993 21:32 ♏ ☌ ☊ ♇ in 4th house. Mag. 0928 SS #123

The eclipse about a month after the start of the event: (The long duration of the eclipse at 6 minutes 14 seconds indicates the ongoing intensity of the massacre.)
   Total ☉ (E) May 10, 1994. 19:49 ♉ in 10th ☍ previous (E) with orb less than 2 degrees.

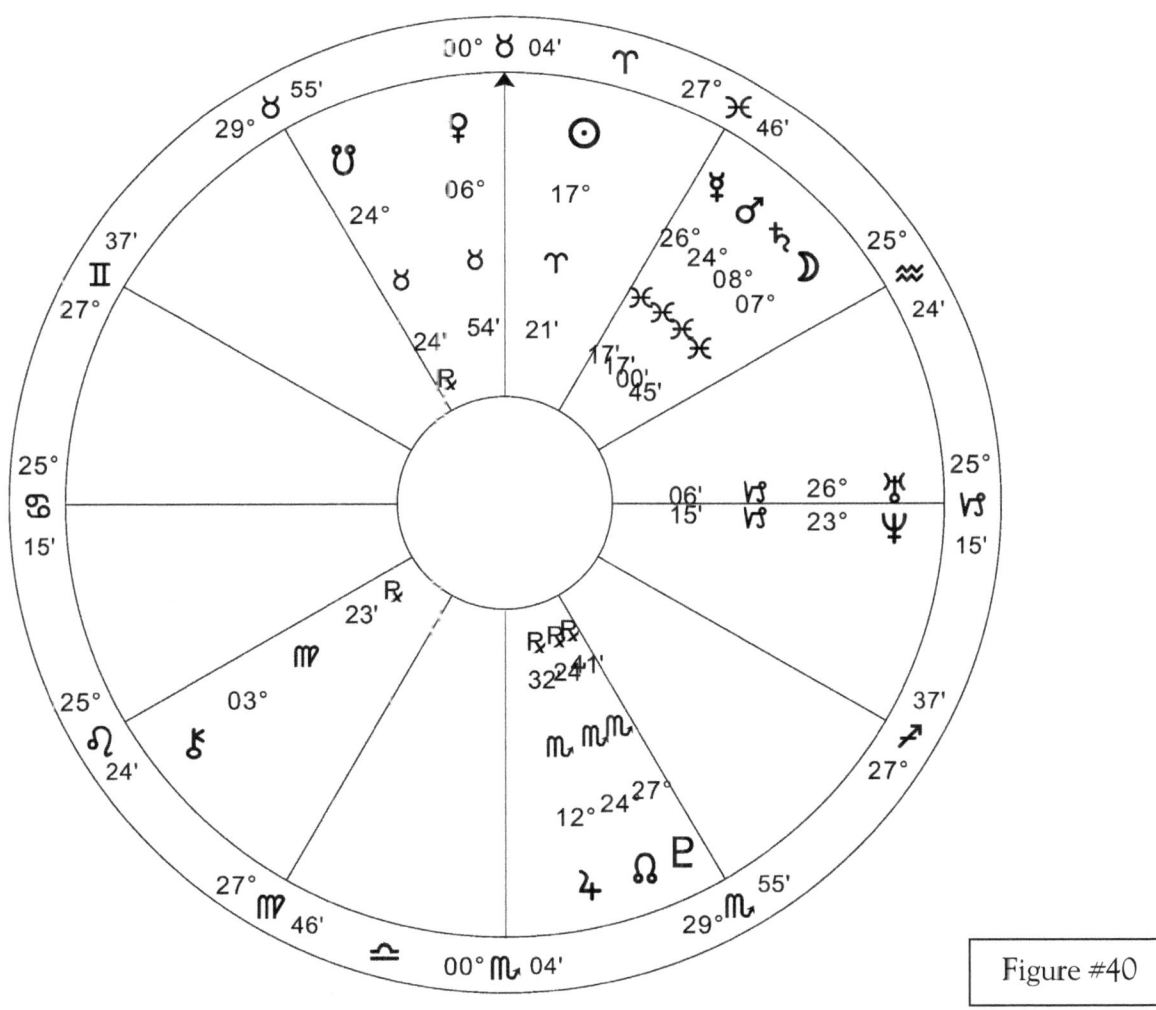

Figure #40

The Columbine High School Massacre: April 20, 1999. 11:19 AM (Figure #41)

Two high school students, Eric Harris and Dylan Klebold, went on a shooting rampage in a high school killing 12 students, 1 teacher, wounding 24 others, and then shooting themselves. Their arsenal included a fire bomb, propane tanks converted to bombs that they put in the cafeteria, 99 other explosive devices and four knives. Their websites included instructions on how to make explosives, pipe bombs, how to cause trouble and various types of death threats. They were indeed troubled and angry teenagers.

GEODETIC CUSPS: For Columbine, Colorado
TWO PREVIOUS ECLIPSES:
  Inner Chart: ANNULAR SOLAR (E) August 22, 1998. Duration 03'14" SS #135
  Outer Chart: ANNULAR SOLAR (E) February 16, 1999. Duration 0'39" SS #140

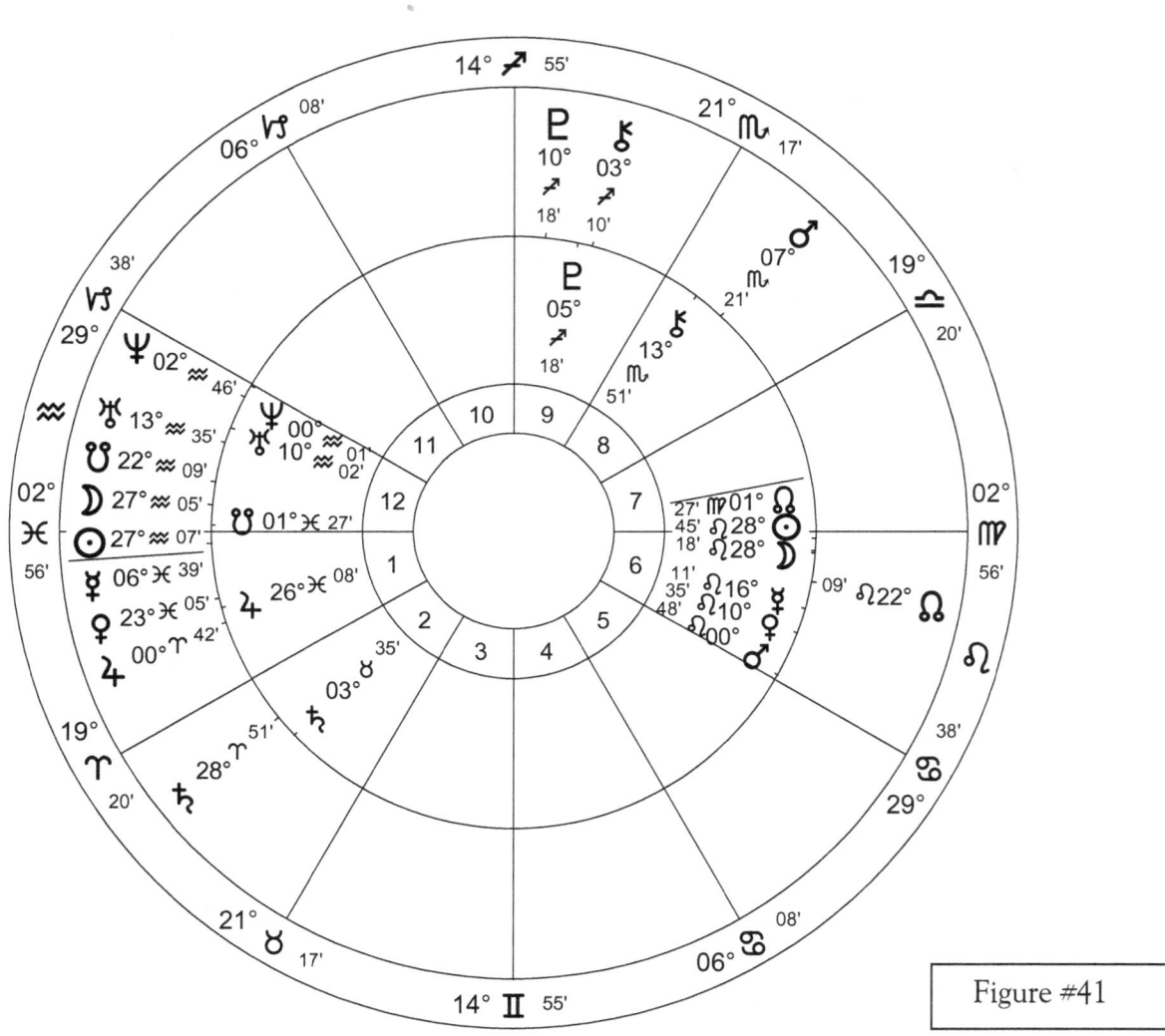

Figure #41

Eclipses are noted on the Ascendant/Descendant angle. Transits on this day include:
Ψ 04:17 ♒ in the 12th, apex a Fixed Sign T-Square with T ♂ ℞ at 05:34 ♏ in the 8th,
☍ ☉/♄ at 00:11 ♉ and 05:53 in the 2nd respectively.
This pattern presaged the Fixed Grand Square in the eclipse pattern of August 11, 1999.

New York Gas Explosion: March 26, 2015. First Alarm at 3:17 pm (Figure #42)

New York's East Village reeled from a devastating gas explosion that was probably caused by a gas line inappropriately tapped into. It was a seven-alarm fire with 250 firefighters on the scene. Three buildings caught fire and collapsed, and twenty-two others were evacuated, including an apartment block. There were six deaths and twenty-two injuries.

In this instance, the chart of the explosion is shown with Geodetic Cusps for New York City. The astrological signature of the event shows Pluto at 15:25 Capricorn directly on the Geodetic Midheaven square Uranus at 15:50 Aries. This is the last of seven exact powerful, revolutionary and transformative Uranus/Pluto squares over a period of three years. It is not always the eclipse patterns that cause devastating events, sometimes it is powerful planetary activity. In this case it is a combination of both the eclipse pair and the exact square of two powerful planets.

PREVIOUS ECLIPSES:
  PARTIAL SOLAR (E) October 23, 2014. 00:24♏. Mag. 0.0811 SS #153 conjunct Descendant
  TOTAL SOLAR (E) March 20, 2015. 29:28♓. Duration 2'47" SS #120 inconjunct Descendant

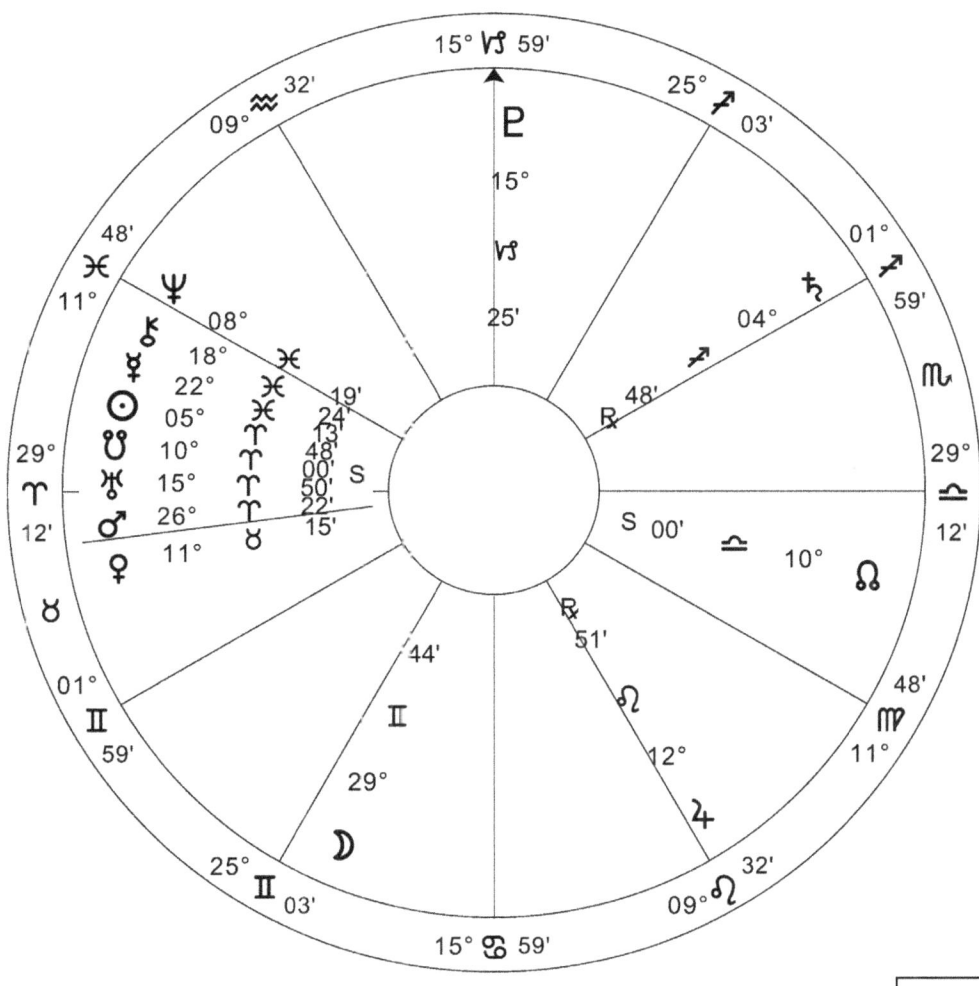

Figure #42

Geodetic Astrology for Relocating and World Affairs

Germanwings Airbus Crash: March 24, 2015 (Figure #43)

Last position 10:53 AM in the French Alps near Digne, France (by French radar)

On this fateful day, Germanwings Airbus 4U9525 left Barcelona, Spain at 10:01 local time, en route to Dusseldorf. Shortly after attaining cruising speed of 38,000 feet the plane started downward and crashed into mountains in the French Alps. All 150 people on board, including 16 children perished. The aircraft was literally ripped apart with no piece intact. Victims were also in the same state of array. The location of the crash was near Digne, France, known as a recreational playground for skiing and hiking, and making rescue work extremely difficult.

    The crash was deemed a deliberate act of sabotage by the co-pilot who had a history of depression. It was possible only because when the captain stepped out of the cockpit the co-pilot locked him out.

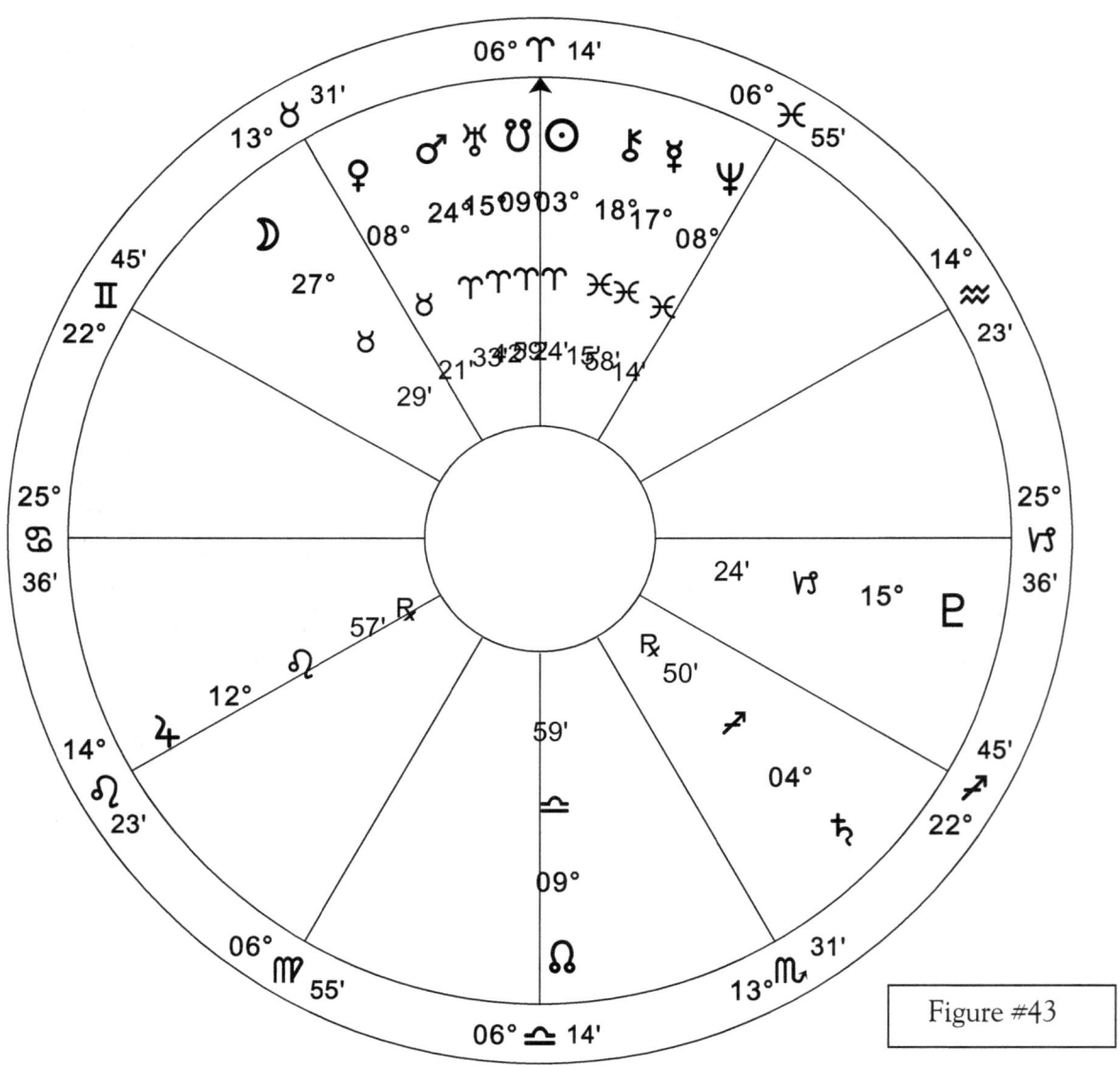

Figure #43

The eclipse pair is in effect the same as in the previous gas explosion disaster in New York.

The eclipse of October 22, 2014 at 00:24 Scorpio is in the fourth house only 6 degrees from the cusp. Note also the position of the Nodes.

The eclipse of March 20, only four days before the crash, at 29:28 Pisces, is in the ninth house just 6 degrees from the Midheaven. Uranus, as it squares Pluto, is posited in the tenth house ruling the eighth of death and destruction.

1929 Stock Market Crash (Figure #44)

When the great money factory of Wall Street collapsed, the rich became paupers and the paupers' dreams of riches were over. Literally hundreds committed suicide and hysteria permeated the air.

It began when people were easily lured to the "fast buck". They flocked all the way up to the Klondike when they heard that gold nuggets were lying on the ground, only to suffer hardship, disappointments and often death. They rushed to the Stock Exchange where easy profit was available. It was "gamblers fever" all across the nation. The rich bought voraciously, keeping the prices rising. Servants, butlers, waitresses, cab drivers and shoe-shiners pricked up their ears and bought stocks that were making the rich richer. They poured in their meager pay cheques, borrowed what they could, then bought on margin. The rising prices were all the security anyone needed. You did not have to rush thousands of miles to the Yukon, or break your back digging in the gravel for nuggets. The only hardship was pushing your way through the throngs flocking to the brokerage offices which had sprung up all across the country, and placing your order.

The new occupation across the nation was watching the miles of ticker tape and cashing in. On Wall Street itself, when morning business began, it seemed that all traffic came to a standstill as throngs of eager buyers flooded the streets, the banking houses and security exchanges. They were only buying paper but as long as profits continued to rise, it was a self-perpetuating process. Dreams of mansions, diamonds and furs camouflaged reality.

When a limit is reached, it only takes a straw to break the proverbial camel's back. On September 5, 1929, a relatively unknown financial adviser named Roger Babson, speaking at a businessman's luncheon, said, "A crash is coming". Word spread rapidly with immediate and disastrous results. The confidence in the market was gone as panic-selling escalated. Investment dealers called in their "tabs" on margin purchases, creating more selling. There were few buyers. By October 21 the ticker tape could not handle the volume and people were ruined long before they even knew it.

By October 24, total bedlam had broken out on Wall Street; people trembled and fainted as fortunes tumbled. It was a bleak day called Black Thursday. Several financiers stepped bravely onto the floor, buying quantities of stocks in a vain attempt to stop the run but fresh money was a signal for frightened investors to keep selling.

By Tuesday, October 29, the panic and hysteria had peaked as people dashed about in a state of daze, trading fortunes on the streets for a dollar, or simply ending their lives. The market lost forty per cent of its value, which was ten times more than the 1929 Federal Budget. Over $100 billion had vanished from the American economy. In today's value that would be over a trillion dollars.

Geodetic Astrology for Relocating and World Affairs

STOCK MARKET CRASH OF 1929
Black Tuesday, October 29, 1929
Geodetic Cusps for New York

Inner Wheel: PARTIAL SOLAR (E) Nov 12, 1928   Mag. 0.808   GMT 9:48:01 SS #122
Outer Wheel: TOTAL SOLAR (E) May 9, 1929   Duration 05'07"   GMT 6:10:10 SS #127

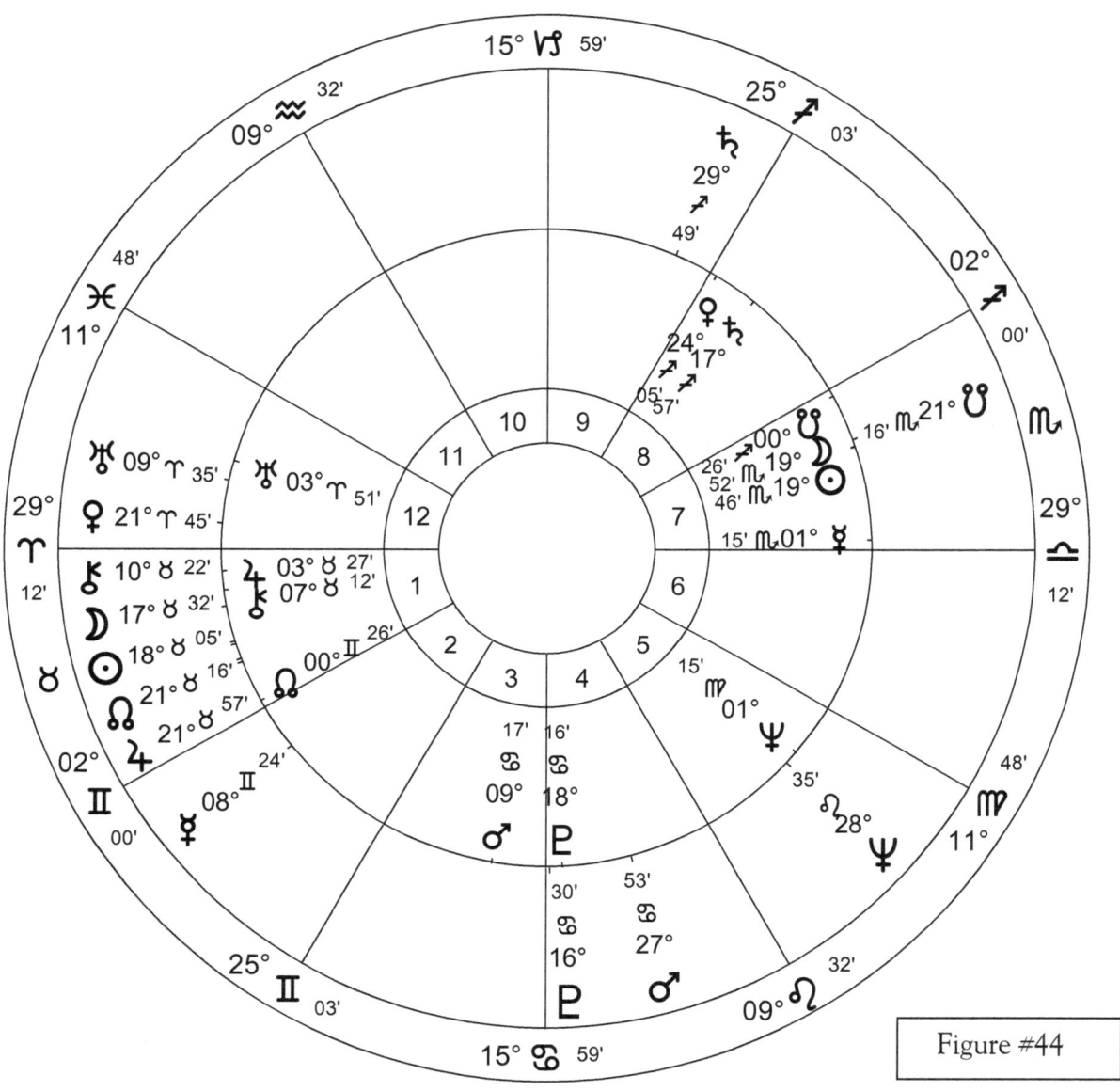

Figure #44

Eclipse ♉/♏ axis – signs ruling money and debt in ☍ with orb of 01:41 across Asc/Desc angle
Eclipse directly before the event, setting the energy:
Note ♃ ☌ ☊ magnifying Jupiter's expansive principle.
Black Thursday: October 24, 1929, ☉ 0:35 ♏ ☌ Descendant at 29°
Transiting ♂ in ♏ from October 7 as action escalated – to November 19 at which time the market and investment panic was over.

It set the direction of the stock market and the economy for a decade to come. It is often considered the start of the Great Depression but it alone was not necessarily the only reason. It destroyed any confidence in the whole economy causing a run on the banks as people withdrew their savings. The banks ran out of cash and were forced to close. When they did re-open they gave depositors ten cents on the dollar.

CHAPTER 7

Summary of Making Geodetic Predictions

Following Geodetic charts and maps over a period of some forty-five years does indicate that it has become a viable framework in which to study world conditions, not necessarily in specific or intricate detail, or precise timing, as much as observing where pressure exists in angles over a period of a few months, waiting for the actual trigger of human action or geophysical slippage.

Part of making an accurate prediction is to determine the range of possibility in a specific area. Once a precise action has begun, it is possible to follow the planetary influences throughout the rest of the event. Determining the trigger moment is much more difficult, if not often impossible or inaccurate.

The same is true in many different kinds of predictions. For example, experience has shown me that during the process of a fatal illness, the actual moment of passing is often impossible to determine because the time period is influenced by a developing cycle coming to its inevitable conclusion. Eclipses and the slower moving planets indicate the frame of time, while the faster planets show shorter influences within the whole. Even the transiting Moon can be a precise trigger to the moment, but its fast movement and short cycle can be likened to a hair trigger on a revolver that comes at a surprising moment; Mars is often a strong trigger on a sensitive part of a chart, and Mercury can sometimes provoke an argument or indicate the timing of a decision.

A distinction should also be made between a prediction and a forecast. A prediction is much more precise but a forecast usually points to an indication or proclivity.

The following is a summary of points to consider in making application through the Geodetic framework:

1. The eclipse "axis" is a major key in making mundane predictions.

    Eclipses often develop in pairs approximately six months apart. Orbs up to ten degrees in opposition or less indicate the potency of that pair as highly influential. Falling across angles or in angular houses also earmarks a location for a special event, be it political, geophysical, or climactic.
    There are exceptions when extreme loss of life or extreme economic loss is concerned, whereby second and eighth houses may be most heavily tenanted.
    Traffic, train or ferry accidents often occur when third and ninth houses are tenanted.

2. There are two exceptions to the above theory:
    (a) When a series of planets on an angle precedes the eclipse in a cadent position, the beginning of the stellium takes precedence.

Summary of Making Geodetic Predictions

(b) When an angular house is either elongated or shortened due to intercepted signs. When a house is elongated the eclipse could still be in the angle that is not easily spotted on the Geodetic map. When a house is considerably smaller than 30 degrees due to intercepted signs the eclipse axis could be in the cadent house prior to the angle but close to the angular cusp.

3. It should be noted if the eclipse is Total, Annular, or Partial.
   Also, the duration of a central eclipse is an important clue as to its potency.
   Some partial eclipses are more potent than others, depending upon how young or old they are; is the eclipse just starting a series at either pole, or is it dwindling off at the end of its long cycle?

4. It is useful to erect a full chart for each eclipse on a flat wheel located at Greenwich.
   A flat wheel puts 0 degrees Aries on the Ascendant followed by 0 degrees of each sign around the houses thereafter. It is a good way to observe planets that may conjunct or oppose the eclipse degree. It also allows observation of aspects or patterns within the context of the whole eclipse chart including squares. The chart can then be relocated to any geographic location desired.

5. The duration of a particular eclipse pair is six months until a new eclipse occurs.

6. The Saros Cycle to which an eclipse belongs could be pertinent.
   The Eagle and the Lark by Bernadette Brady gives the first eclipse in each series and describes its influence. You will have to search for each eclipse according to its degree because the numbering system does not follow the NASA system as previously described.

   The oldest Saros Series running at this time is #117. SS #116 finished on July 22, 1971.
   The youngest Saros Cycle #156 started July 1, 2011 at 9:21 Cancer with a very slight amount of the Sun's diameter obscured at 0.097.

7. Transiting lunations act as either reinforcement of the influence or as a trigger.

8. Observe transiting Great Conjunctions as they add further influence. Details can be found in *Tables of Planetary Phenomena*.

9. A planet in its perigee adds to its strength.
   That came to attention when Pluto was in Scorpio, which is at its closest point to earth in its very long cycle. The Moon in perigee adds intensity as a potential trigger.

10. Any aspect can act as a trigger, especially a conjunction, but the opposition, square and quincunx can trigger with equal effectiveness. Sextiles seem to occur more frequently than trines. It could be said that the sextile is an opportunity for an event to happen.

11. T-Square configurations are especially dangerous, more so in Fixed signs, and more so if a planet squares both eclipses.

12. Declinations should be noted, particularly if a planet is turning at one of the solstices. It is a short standstill position that can be stronger due to the concentrated duration of its influence.
    Also a planet turning retrograde at either equinox can cause an 'anomaly' as previously described. Its planetary longitude does not match its north or south direction from the Celestial Equator. (See Figure #28.)

13. Any planet can act as a trigger.

    Mars hastens
    Jupiter magnifies, not protects
    Neptune is often prominent in both earthquakes and volcanic eruptions
    Uranus amplifies
    Pluto compounds

14. A stationary planet is particularly sensitive in an eclipse chart. This is also true in a transit affecting the situation. Even the act of slowing down to approach a stationary position increases the potency of the influence.

15. Any planet conjunct or square the Nodes increases the extent or influence of the situation.

16. Planets in their dignity or exaltation increase their energy.

17. Some Fixed Stars are particularly effective. More attention should be paid to these.

18. Due to the sophistication of our computer programs, we can easily determine the path of any eclipse. It is evident that an event does not have to be under the shadow of an eclipse for it to happen but it does seem to add intensity.

CHAPTER 8

Guide for Construction of a Geodetic World Map

This involves a bit of work but it is well worth the effort if you do any amount of this kind of astrology. Having a map on a wall in your office makes it easy to follow transits and shifting eclipse patterns. It also makes it easy to see where any planet in a client's chart is angular, particularly if it is one that is better handled as an internal processing journey for them. This is helpful if a client is planning a vacation and is curious as to its influences. As previously stated, a permanent change of residence requires much more precise charting.

Select a large map about 2½ feet by 4 feet. This allows for both ease and relative accuracy in finding the close approximations of the Midheavens and Ascendants of any location in the world. Rand McNally issues a good one that is quite accurate and uncluttered. Degrees of longitude need to be marked at the top and latitude down the side. I have a large colored one, as well as a smaller one about 11 inches by 17 inches that I copied from an atlas and marked the angles with a highlighter. It is very handy for travelling and packs easily with conference papers.

The preference, of course, is always to cast a complete Geodetic chart.

Each Midheaven is Marked Across the Top
Each Midheaven is laid out from Greenwich at 30° intervals, commencing at 0° moving in an easterly direction.

    Example:
        0° longitude   = 0° Aries
        30° East longitude   = 0° Taurus
        60° East longitude   = 0° Gemini, etc.

    You can also back up from Greenwich for each sign
        30° West longitude   = 0° Pisces
        60° West longitude   = 0° Aquarius
        90° West longitude   = 0° Capricorn, etc.

    There will be twelve equal divisions of 30 degrees each, one for each sign of the zodiac consecutively. These signs can be shown across the top but cover the entire vertical area. Draw your vertical lines down the map from the top to the bottom for each 30 degrees division.
    Use a colored highlighter pen, preferably pink so it stands out but does not obliterate anything on your map.

Ascendant Divisions

The Ascendant lines are shown in Figure #45 (p. 106) by dotted lines. These dotted lines indicate zero degrees of each Ascendant, moving from left to right. Once drawn in it is easy to ascertain the whole 30 degrees of each Ascendant and portions thereof.

Using the tables given below, at each latitude given, and at the point where it crosses the given Midheaven, mark an 'X'. Choose the appropriate degree for the Midheaven as close as possible. On a larger map this can be done with reasonable accuracy.

When all the 'X' points for zero degrees of that Ascendant have been marked, connect them with a line. Use Figure #45 as your guide.

Aries Ascendant
Draw a line straight down 90° West longitude. That whole line is both 0° Capricorn Midheaven and 0° Aries Ascendant.

Libra Ascendant
Draw a line straight down 90° East longitude. That whole line is both 0° Cancer Midheaven and 0° Libra Ascendant.

Taurus Ascendant

Lat.	MC	Asc
60 N	07 Capricorn	00 Taurus
45 N	16 Capricorn	" "
30 N	20 Capricorn	" "
15 N	23 Capricorn	" "
0	26 Capricorn	" "
15 S	29 Capricorn	" "
30 S	02 Aquarius	" "
45 S	07 Aquarius	" "
60 S	16 Aquarius	" "

Gemini Ascendant

Lat.	MC	Asc
60 N	16 Capricorn	00 Gemini
45 N	04 Aquarius	" "
30 N	13 Aquarius	" "
15 N	19 Aquarius	" "
0	26 Aquarius	" "
15 S	2-1/2 Pisces	" "
30 S	08 Pisces	" "
45 S	18 Pisces	" "
60 S	18 Aries	" "

Cancer Ascendant

Lat	MC	Asc
60 N	09 Aquarius	00 Cancer
45 N	03 Pisces	" "
30 N	14 Pisces	" "
15 N	23 Pisces	" "
0	00 Aries	" "
15 S	07 Aries	" "
30 S	16 Aries	" "
45 S	27 Aries	" "

Leo Ascendant

Lat	MC	Asc
60 N	22 Pisces	00 Leo
45 N	10 Aries	" "
30 N	21 Aries	" "
15 N	29 Aries	" "
0	05 Taurus	" "
15 S	10 Taurus	" "
30 S	17 Taurus	" "
45 S	26 Taurus	" "

Guide for Construction of a Geodetic World Map

Virgo Ascendant

Lat	MC	Asc
60 N	14 Taurus	00 Virgo
45 N	23 Taurus	" "
30 N	28 Taurus	" "
15 N	01 Gemini	" "
0	05 Gemini	" "
15 S	07 Gemini	" "
30 S	10 Gemini	" "
45 S	15 Gemini	" "

Scorpio Ascendant

Lat	MC	Asc
60 N	16 Leo	00 Scorpio
45 N	08 Leo	" "
30 N	02 Leo	" "
15 N	29 Cancer	" "
0	26 Cancer	" "
15 S	23 Cancer	" "
30 S	19 Cancer	" "
45 S	14 Cancer	" "

Sagittarius Ascendant

Lat	MC	Asc
60 N	08 Libra	00 Sag
45 N	19 Virgo	" "
30 N	09 Virgo	" "
15 N	01 Virgo	" "
0	25 Leo	" "
15 S	20 Leo	" "
30 S	13 Leo	" "
45 S	04 Leo	" "
60 S	24 Cancer	" "

Capricorn Ascendant

Asc	MC	Asc
60 N	20 Scorpio	00 Cap
45 N	27 Libra	" "
30 N	16 Libra	" "
15 N	07 Libra	" "
0	00 Libra	" "
15 S	23 Virgo	" "
30 S	15 Virgo	" "
45 S	03 Virgo	" "
60 S	09 Leo	" "

Aquarius Ascendant

Lat	MC	Asc
60 N	13 Sag	00 Aqu
45 N	26 Scorpio	" "
30 N	17 Scorpio	" "
15 N	10 Scorpio	" "
0	05 Scorpio	" "
15 S	29 Libra	" "
30 S	21 Libra	" "
45 S	12 Libra	" "
60 S	22 Virgo	" "

Pisces Ascendant

Lat	MC	Asc
60 N	23 Sag	00 Pisces
45 N	15 Sag	" "
30 N	10 Sag	" "
15 N	07 Sag	" "
0	04 Sag	" "
15 S	01 Sag	" "
30 S	27 Scorpio	" "
45 S	23 Scorpio	" "

GUIDE FOR CONSTRUCTION OF GEODETIC MAP - TROPICAL PLACIDUS TABLE OF HOUSES

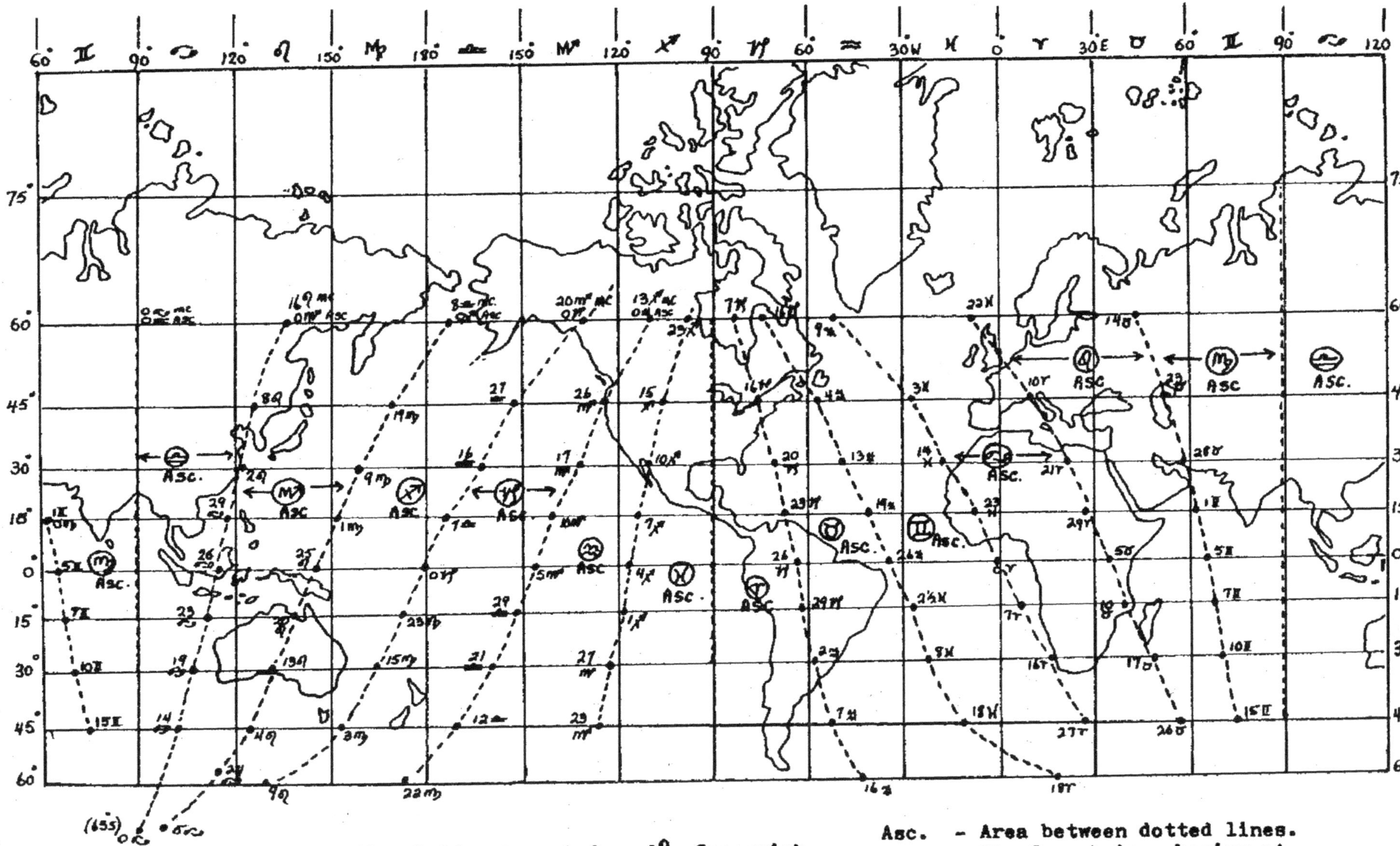

Asc. - Area between dotted lines.
0° of each Asc. begins at dotted line moving left to right

M.C. positions are given for 0° of Ascendants, at various latitudes.

M.C. - Zodiac laid out east from 0° Greenwich
- 12 Equal Divisions of 30°
- Shown across top but covers complete area from north to south

Figure #45

BIBLIOGRAPHY

Baigent, Michael; Campion, Nicholas; Harvey, Charles, *Mundane Astrology, An Introduction to the Astrology of Nations and Groups*, Aquarian Press 1984

Carter, Charles E.O., *Introduction to Political Astrology*, L.N. Fowler & Co. Ltd., London

Davis, Martin. Ed., *From Here to There, An Astrologer's Guide to Astromapping*, The Wessex Astrologer, Bournemouth, 2008

McRae, I.I. Chris, *The Geodetic World Map*, American Federation of Astrologers, Tempe, Arizona, 1988

Meadows, David, *Where in the World with Astro*Carto*Graphy*, American Federation of Astrologers Tempe, Arizona, 1998

Michelsen, Neil F., *Tables of Planetary Phenomena*, Third Edition, Starcrafts Publishing, Exeter, NH, 2007

Nash, Jay Robert, *The Darkest Hour*, Wallaby Edition, New York, 1977

Sepharial, *The Geodetic Equivalent*, American Federation of Astrologers, Tempe, Arizona, 1972

News Sources

'Great Moments of the Century', As Reported by the *New York Times*, Arno Press, New York, 1977

Newspaper articles clipped from *The Edmonton Journal*

Wikipedia, http://wikipedia.org

Other Titles from The Wessex Astrologer
www.wessexastrologer.com

Martin Davis	Astrolocality Astrology / From Here to There
Wanda Sellar	The Consultation Chart / An Introduction to Medical Astrology / Introduction to Decumbiture
Geoffrey Cornelius	The Moment of Astrology
Darrelyn Gunzburg	Life After Grief / AstroGraphology: The Hidden Link between your Horoscope and your Handwriting
Paul F. Newman	Declination: The Steps of the Sun / Luna: The Book of the Moon
Jamie Macphail	Astrology and the Causes of War
Deborah Houlding	The Houses: Temples of the Sky
Dorian Geiseler Greenbaum	Temperament: Astrology's Forgotten Key
Howard Sasportas	The Gods of Change
Patricia L. Walsh	Understanding Karmic Complexes
M. Kelly Hunter	Living Lilith
Barbara Dunn	Horary Astrology Re-Examined
Deva Green	Evolutionary Astrology
Jeff Green	Pluto Volume 1 / Pluto Volume 2 / Essays on Evolutionary Astrology (ed. by Deva Green)
Dolores Ashcroft-Nowicki and Stephanie V. Norris	The Door Unlocked: An Astrological Insight into Initiation
Martha Betz	The Betz Placidus Table of Houses
Greg Bogart	Astrology and Meditation
Kim Farnell	Flirting with the Zodiac
Henry Seltzer	The Tenth Planet
Ray Grasse	Under a Sacred Sky
Martin Gansten	Primary Directions
Joseph Crane	Astrological Roots: The Hellenistic Legacy / Between Fortune and Providence
John Gadbury	The Nativity of the Late King Charles
Komilla Sutton	The Essentials of Vedic Astrology / The Lunar Nodes / Personal Panchanga / The Nakshatras
Anthony Louis	The Art of Forecasting using Solar Returns
Lorna Green	Your Horoscope in Your Hands
Reina James	All the Sun Goes Round
Oscar Hofman	Classical Medical Astrology
Bernadette Brady	Astrology, A Place in Chaos / Star and Planet Combinations
Richard Idemon	The Magic Thread / Through the Looking Glass
Nick Campion	The Book of World Horoscopes
Judy Hall	Patterns of the Past / Karmic Connections / Good Vibrations / The Soulmate Myth / The Book of Why / Book of Psychic Development
Neil D. Paris	Surfing your Solar Cycles
Michele Finey	The Sacred Dance of Venus and Mars
David Hamblin	The Spirit of Numbers
Dennis Elwell	Cosmic Loom
Gillian Helfgott	The Insightful Turtle
Christina Rose	The Tapestry of Planetary Phases
Bob Makransky	Planetary Strength / Planetary Hours / Planetary Combination

www.ingramcontent.com/pod-product-compliance
Lightning Source LLC
Chambersburg PA
CBHW081135170426
43197CB00017B/2868